Speaking in Tongues of the Woke Left

A Metamodern Deconstruction of the New Faith

SEAN DEMPSEY

EDITED BY:
DANIEL NORONHA

ISBN: 9798303965362

Copyright © 2024 Sean Dempsey

ALL RIGHTS RESERVED.
No part of this publication may be reproduced, distributed, or transmitted in any form or by any means, including photocopying, recording, or other electronic or mechanical methods, without the prior written permission of the publisher, except in the case of brief quotations embodied in critical reviews and certain other noncommercial uses permitted by copyright law.

DEDICATION

To my daughter. May she one day grow up in a world full of hope and devoid of madness.

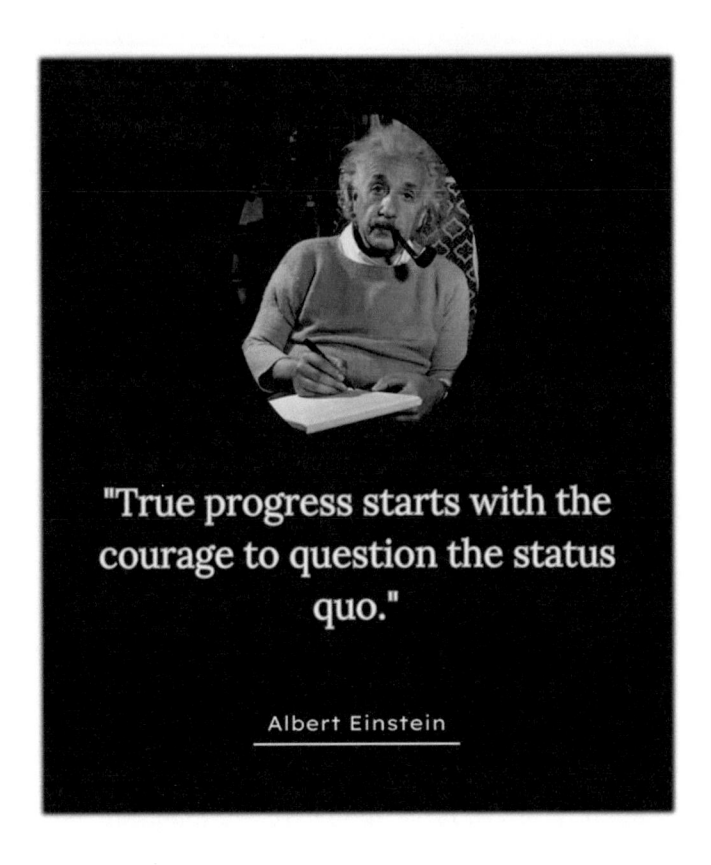

> "True progress starts with the courage to question the status quo."
>
> Albert Einstein

> ...the Holy Spirit came on all who heard the message. The circumcised believers who had come with Peter were astonished that the gift of the Holy Spirit had been poured out even on Gentiles. For they heard them *speaking in tongues* and praising God.
>
> *Acts 10:44-46*

TABLE OF CONTENTS

DEDICATION .... *iii*
PREFACE *1*
INTRODUCTION *5*
FAITH (/fāTH/). noun. *17*

    Blind Faith.. 19
    Faith is a Currency................................. 21
    A Woke God.. 23
    The Third Rails: Religion & Politics 24
        The Faith/Identity Entanglement Problem 25
        The Differing Value Systems Problem..................... 25
        The Cognitive Bias Problem 27
    "Normal" Thinking 31
    The Golden Idol..................................... 34
    Metamorphosis of Faith 36

WHAT IS WOKE? *37*

    Woke History 37
    Woke Stolen from the Black Community 40
    Shifting Meaning of Words.................. 42
    Sermon Recap 45

DIALECTIC BREAKDOWN & FORMING SYNTHESIS *47*

    Pre-Modernity 48
    Modernity... 49

- Postmodernism 49
- Metamodernism 50
- Postmodernism's Architype 50
- Dialectical Synthesis (Gender Example) 52
- Metamorphosis 53

THE HIERARCHY OF OPPRESSION 55
- Ranking Oppression 56
- The Hierarchy in Action 59
- Woke Diagnosis 62

IDENTITY POLITICS, WHITE PRIVILEGE, & RACISM 63
- The Paragon of Wokeness 63
- Is MLK's Dream Dead in the Woke Church? 65

OPPRESSION OF WOMEN 76
- The Women's Right Movement 77
- Tensions Within Feminism 79
- Expanding Feminist Goals 80

TRANSGENDERISM 82
- Transgenderism Defined 83
- Transgenderism Harms LGB & Feminism 84
- Interview of Timothy Baxter 86
- Closing Thoughts 92

WALL STREET "GOES WOKE" 93

    The 1% vs the 99% 93

    Turning of the Tide... 94

    Timeline of Events.. 95

    Correlation Speculation...................................... 99

    Interview of Kevin Maley 100

CASE IN POINT: WOKE HYSTERIA **113**

    Corrupted Language... 113

    War on Words.. 116

    Legal Challenges.. 118

    An Appeal to Common Sense? 121

WOKE BLOWBACK & WOKE REVULSION **122**

    Gender Affirming Care 124

    Woke Irony 129

THE WOKE RIGHT ***131***

    The Woke Right Won't Cancel Out The Woke Left
.... 135

A REASON FOR GREAT OPTIMISM ***136***

    Interview of Brendan Dempsey 137

ABOUT THE AUTHOR ***154***

OTHER PUBLISHED WORKS ***154***

PREFACE

You may be curious – so why did I write this book? No, I don't have any spiritual or political axes to grind. No, I don't wish to tilt at windmills. This book is not some manifesto of righteous judgements or one-sided anecdotes. Rather, I wrote this book for one simple reason: because **political division is tearing our country apart** and neither "side" has any interest in listening to the other.

Sadly, very few individuals are forming opinions or shaping their viewpoints based on their core values and then allowing those beliefs to drive corresponding placement into a political party or social grouping. Instead, it is the exact opposite! By and large, the PARTY sets the direction and then expects its dutiful members to step into line and salute whatever dogma is being touted. In short, the *status quo* is the compliance of obedient lap dogs.

This conformity is by no means one-sided. CNN and MSNBC rant about the evils of the "Alt-Right Racist MAGA Supporters;" Fox News spouts the evils of the "Dirty Dems" and "Woke Left." If Trump or his cabinet is for something, the Left is righteously against it. If the Democrats love a thing, the Right is righteously against it. Neither side spends much time espousing what it is *for*, but delights in decrying what it is *against*. It is an exhausting game of partisanship which leaves much of the country devoid of hope and frustrated with politics.

No single term better encapsulates this deep divide than the term "Woke." The word is a vile pejorative on the Right—derided and ridiculed. The word is a rallying cry for the Progressive Left—who have made it a beacon of hope for the underserved and oppressed. Because this single word is so greatly misunderstood (by both sides), it demands interrogation and study.

Additionally, as the Woke "movement" is a direct byproduct of postmodernism, there is opportunity for macro-level analysis of the over-arching framework and the complex stratification at play. In short, this *single word* – this demon to the Right and lodestar to the Left – is so pregnant with meaning that it seems to break under its own weight. It is the perfect case study for Postmodern thought.

The goal for this book is to find common ground. Both "sides" are so busy screaming at each other and going deaf in their echo chambers that they cannot conceivably hear each other, much less carry on a rational dialogue. There is some good in the goals of the Woke movement, yet valid reason for the visceral backlash. When one side feels that they are not being listened to (or are having unsterilized doctrine forced down their throat) it can foster extreme resentment and pushback.

It is undeniable that one side of the argument completely dominates the media, the collegiate halls of academia, the supermajority of professional "corporate" news outlets, and almost all of entertainment ("Hollywood"). In the face of so much preaching, it's no surprise that there is a counterreaction commensurate to the helplessness created on the other side.

It is perhaps a great irony that the Woke movement – by definition, impassioned with concerns about diversity and inclusion – has historically seemed disinterested in allowing *diversity of thought* or alternative viewpoints. The political Right has been left out in the cold, unable to properly express its counterarguments. As a result, the backlash to Wokeism is extreme and becomes wildly polarized. Woke becomes the supervillain: a cartoonish fiend to galvanize Right-wing supporters against the Left.

Meanwhile, the Left, in its deafening echo chamber, instills Wokeism as its choice religion, complete with spiritual iconography and a lexicon to match its station. Thus, a great bifurcation forms and then spins out of control; both camps retreat to their respective sides so they can hurl insults and vitriol at the other across a deep political chasm.

The nihilist would expect this outcome. Division is perhaps humanity's *sine qua non*. The pessimist expects mankind to be forever lost in its own resentments and loathing.

But this book shares an alternate take. Even now, at the pinnacle of distrust and insanity across both sides of the political aisle, there is reason for optimism, for a m*etamodern dialectical synthesis* is forming between the warring factions of Modernity and Postmodernism and its prime archetype, *Wokeism*. From out of this contest will emerge a whole greater than the sum of its parts. The sick deadwood may need to burn to the ground, but from the ashes will grow a lush forest.

A revival of introspection and learning is coming. There is light at the end of this dark tunnel. The Postmodern era and, with it, the milieu of Woke ideology, is deconstructive by nature—so it seeks to defame and destroy; that is its *causa prima* ("main purpose" or "first cause"). Postmodernism has been in the driver's seat for the last several decades. This is why our world feels so unhinged and fragmented. But a new era of thought and solidarity is around the corner...

We stand nearer than we might think to a new epoch of spiritual and cultural enlightenment. This North Star, and all that it stands for, should be a beacon of hope. I wish to deconstruct Wokeism so we can explore that brighter future together. It is for this reason I wrote this book.

"The trouble with the world is that the stupid are cocksure and the intelligent are full of doubt."
— ***Bertrand Russell***

INTRODUCTION

Before getting into the meat and potatoes of this treatise, I thought I'd talk a little about myself. How fun! My first memories begin in northern Vermont, which is where I spent my days with two younger brothers, climbing steep rockfaces in the woods and making bizarre home videos with a handheld 8mm camcorder the way only a family of home-schooled children in the backwoods of Vermont truly can.

I was a church-going kid and grew up in a religious family. I listened exclusively to Christian music. I was not allowed to watch R-rated movies. Life was structured yet rich, fun, and enjoyable.

I was 12 years old. The year was 1996. I was VERY into computers. I was more than a bit of a geek. Heck, what do you expect from a home-schooled kid? Looking back, I can say that my self-directed education made me who I am today—for better or for worse. Eventually, a new sister joined our family, and a few years later I started attending a private school located an hour south.

Around this time, I remember an exciting Protestant "revival" began to roll out in my fertile, green state. I guess I should say at this point in my life the Dempseys were members of the *Assemblies of God* family of Protestant churches. This revival started in Toronto, Canada and was part of something called *The Toronto Blessing.* Essentially, the raw and unfiltered Holy Spirit—the one that leads to uncontrollable laughter, speaking in tongues, and erratic gyrating—descended south from Toronto and laid siege to the northern US states. This phenomenon began to make waves as Christians from all over came to experience the highly charged and erratic church services in my home state, and my church community of Saint Albans was similarly consumed by the spiritual electricity of the moment.

Like a power toggle was pressed, the once-boring weekly church services turned quite interesting. While I would be lying if I said I recalled all the specifics, I do clearly remember various occasions of haphazard laughter (this was called "Holy laughter") breaking out randomly during worship—as well as people like my friend's mother twitching her hands uncontrollably and then needing to be led to the floor where she stayed for the remainer of our pastor's sermon (aka she was "Slain in the Spirit").

The memory is particularly vivid because of the warring thoughts inside my brain. I recall being completely unable to pay attention to the service as I was busy asking myself if God preferred His children to listen to the preacher's lesson—or to be passed out on the floor transfixed in ecstatic rapture? I was far too young to describe myself as being cynical, but I remember thinking she might have simply dozed off with complete immunity. If the pile carpet wasn't so rough, I might even have envied her.

These services weren't just a fad. They spread like divine wildfire. As with geese in the winter, God's divine presence had a way of heading south. Before I knew it, the *real* intense God services were being held not in St. Albans (which is a mere twenty-two miles from the Canadian border) but in Burlington Vermont!

A few months later my father asked me if I'd like to go to an evening "revival meeting" (as they were called) in Burlington. This was pretty exciting for me. I had never been to one before; I'd only tasted a shadow of what the "real" revival meetings were like when folks like my overweight neighbor, Mr. McChuckles *(name changed for privacy)* would violently shake, speak in tongues, and be unable to sing during worship due to a fit of wild laughter. But a REAL evening revival session sounded awesome.

At this time, I was a passionate and self-professing Christian – but what might be considered (by many in my circles) as an 'unsanctified' Christian. I was nearly 13. But I had never spoken in tongues! I had never shaken uncontrollably. I had never felt my hands or legs jitter with the fear or joy of God. I had never even fainted and had His all-consuming love wash over me as I laid prostrate on the ground. I was just one of those "I believe in God" Christians. I was a boring "I need His grace" type of Christian. But I wanted more. I needed more. I just had to have more faith! I'd surely find that in the revival meeting…

Heading out that Friday night, we arrived in Burlington approximately forty-five minutes later. I remember the parking lot was PACKED. Dad told me people were still coming from all over the country and even from Canada. "God is really putting Vermont on the map," he told me with excitement. I jumped out of the car after we found a spot way in the back and walked in.

Immediately the energy changed. There was dancing. Singing. People were on the ground all around the room. There were folks being gently dragged to central areas by designated "people movers" (at least as I referred to them in my mind). The music was surprisingly loud. The place was packed! We slipped into a pew in the back and began to participate in the worship session. The service apparently had been going on for a while, even though I don't think we were late. Someone near the front of the stage had an elk antler-shaped horn and was blowing into it regularly. This was like nothing I had ever experienced before. God was surely in this room!

The music eventually quieted, and a preacher began to preach. It was a loud and boisterous sermon, but I don't remember a word of it. I know "revival" was mentioned a lot, as was "the spirit of God" and His "all-consuming fire." It was mesmerizing. When the sermon ended, the preacher asked if anyone wanted to receive a blessing and prayer up front. More than half the room left their seats and started to form queues. My father stood up and got in a newly formed line.

I swallowed hard. Then, before I knew it, I was out of my chair and looking for a spot in line near the left side of the room.

The music started back up, and with it frenzied and bizarre-looking dancing. The man with the elk horn had left the stage and was starting to work his way into the pews. Men and women were all around me, twitching and shaking. Wild sounds were coming from their lips as they shouted words no one could understand (this was the point – only God could understand the invented languages). Like the beaches of Normandy, people were dropping all around me in their pews while I progressed forward. As people fell to the ground beside me to the left and to the right, they were dragged quietly to other areas of the room, to be *Slain in the Spirit* and lay together. Some of them bobbed with little electric movements as they languished on the patterned red carpet; others wildly laughed as they lay face-up, eyes closed. Still others were perfectly still, as if dead.

I swallowed again. It was my turn to receive prayer next. To be clear, "receiving prayer" was a euphemism in the revival circuit. Men and women up toward the front were praying for those who met them. The expectation was for you to approach them, open up your hands, close your eyes, and explain what you sought God to do in your life. Then the prayer would start, but it was your responsibility to be so completely and utterly taken by the Holy Spirit that you lost all control of your body. You were expected to tip and to weave—bob and bend in the presence of the Spirit of God. Here at a revival session, you were also *expected* to speak in tongues! It was hardly optional. The Holy Spirit was in this room, so His mighty power would grip you and make you speak directly to Him, but in a language that only He could understand. If you were lucky, the person who was praying with you or beside you could then interpret the prayer, but this was only if he or she had the Spiritual Gift of *Interpretation*. Not everyone had the requisite gift; so, most of the tongues went uninterpreted. After all this, you would then fall to the ground and be Slain in the Spirit.

The man with the elk horn was way behind me but I could hear him getting closer. He was really going to town on that thing! It didn't really fit the beat of the music, but that didn't stop him. As the person in front of me receiving prayer started speaking in tongues, his legs buckled, and he went down like a lump of potatoes. Another man in a blue robe (a church deacon no doubt) was there to receive his pulsating body and drag him over to a corner. I stepped forward to receive my blessing.

I'll never forget to my dying day what happened next. It was a profound moment in my life. Here I was ready and willing to receive the full power of God and have the Holy Spirit literally knock me to the ground and speak new languages in His name. So, what happened?

Nothing.

Well, not exactly nothing. First, I exchanged a few words with the person who I was praying with, and then let him know it was my first time at a revival meeting, and that I had never spoken in tongues before. He then told me that only the Blessed Divine speak in tongues and reverently invited me to be *filled with the Holy Spirit*! So, I tried.

Man, did I try!

I prayed with him. I opened my heart. I told God to use me. The man I was praying with began to speak loudly in tongues, turning on his secret God-language like a light bulb. "Ela paiya-el dora el peshria elle dea fiay es ela misa pora DIMA EL SAYA TIMA LIMA FIMA GRIMA DRIMA" *et cetera*. Of course I don't remember a word the man really said, but for the sake of the narrative, it was something like that. I kept my eyes closed so tight that tears started to come out of them, and I opened my mouth and tried to feel the power of God run through me. But it didn't. And I didn't make a sound. I thought, just for a moment, of trying to fake the words and imitate the people I was near. But I quickly stopped myself, believing that there could probably be no worse sin than feigning a spiritual blessing. After a few minutes of me awkwardly standing there, unwavering in my inability to invent a new language—and physically unwavering as I stood on two feet and refusing to acquiesce to the raw, unfiltered Spirit that would cause my limbs to start shaking—the man started to gently push my head. Then the pushing became more intense. His voice picked up as he spoke in the Spirit of uninterpreted, holy tongues, and he would shout "EL LIMA FLA SHIMA" really loudly as he pushed on my head. Finally, he pushed so hard that I stumbled backwards and fell into the arms of the robed man waiting to receive my limp torso.

I then did something I'm not especially proud of. I went with it.

I let the body snatcher deacon drag me to the area with other slain Christian warriors. Eyes closed, I felt myself grow further from the elk horn and closer to warm bodies lying on the floor. There was crying all around me, as well as hysterical laughing. I heard the thumping of contorting bodies flailing against the hard, thin carpeting. And I laid there with them. Eyes shut, pretending to be immovable due to the hand of God pressed against my body—preventing me from rising until I had emotionally and psychologically wrestled with God like Jacob physically did.

Lying on that cheap red church carpet, eyes closed, my mind raced. Was I unworthy of His touch? Was there something about me that was so defective that He didn't want to use me or speak through me? Was I so defiant to the way of the almighty God that He refused to use me as His vessel?

The man with the elk horn suddenly sounded it loudly next to me, and I opened my eyes. It was hard to see at first; they had tears in them.

Eventually I got up from the icy church floor and made it back to my seat. My father was there praying. The service ended not long after, and we left.

I don't remember anything about the ride home. I don't remember if we spoke a word. I don't think we did. In any case, I left that church service *hollowed out* and more confused than at any prior time in my life. Did I not have enough faith? Did I have *any* faith?

*   *   *

Many years later I graduated from high school and enrolled at the University of Vermont. The first year was a blur and not worth mentioning (other than the fact I met and connected with people there who would become lifelong friends and family). In my second year, however, I became a Resident Advisor ("RA"). This was another life-changing experience for me.

Interestingly enough, the reason why becoming an RA was so profound for me had nothing to do with the actual responsibilities of *being an RA*, nor the virtues of working with students. That part I found extremely easy (and rewarding). The part that was so provocative about this experience was the *training* to become an RA. RA training was a complete paradigm shift for me as a person. It rocked me to my core.

I was 19ish years old now, and still fairly impressionable. It takes more than a few semesters of college to wipe away the forced innocence of multiple years of home-schooling. Yet, during this time, I began to soak up like a sponge all the knowledge and information that RA training imparted. It was a 2-week training program with grueling 8-to-10 hours per day spent in immersive learning exercises. Highly educated and published speakers were brought in for lengthy seminars and day-long sessions, employed with intricate games and robust exercises used to convey and drive home the salient topics. Ironically enough, the training we went through consisted of very little information pertaining to what I initially thought might be important. Yes, we covered situations involving serious incidents and even conducted role playing around alcohol and drug overdoes and how to respond. But, in truth, this sort of 'practical' hands-on knowledge represented less than 1% of our training. The vast majority of RA training was learning about diversity, systematic oppression, the roles of the oppressor vs the oppressed, and the importance of one's group identity in framing their view of the world. We studied how our gender, race, and ethnicity were critical drivers of our success or failures. I also learned about the inherent dangers of whiteness and how being a white, cis, male essentially ushered me to the top of the Privilege Pyramid. The greatest threats to dignity and society were sexism, racism, ageism, classism, ableism, heterosexism, and all other "isms," which served as a way for oppressors to further oppress minorities and those without the same level of power.

I found these concepts absolutely fascinating. I asked a myriad of questions. In many ways, much of what I had believed to the true before was now breaking down. For example, prior to this point in my life, I had thought that capitalism was a means for allowing anyone in the country to achieve prosperity and "pull themselves up by their bootstraps;" however, in these RA training courses I now learned that capitalism was a framework of systemic oppression used to maintain the asymmetrical power dynamics by white power brokers. Capitalism thus disproportionally disenfranchised oppressed minorities and uniquely benefited privileged whites.

Even seemingly innocuous parts of life I soon learned to be examples of oppression. I remember late in one open session the following exchange took place:

> **Lecturer**: "...and that is why most Band-Aids all are colored pinkish white: because the capitalist power brokers are reaffirming that brown and black persons don't really fit in – not truly – in this society. It is yet another flagrant example of top-down oppression and racism."
>
> My hand went up at this point.
>
> **Lecturer**: "Yes. May I help you?"
>
> **Me**: "Yes, thank you; I'm sorry to interject. I just have a quick question. In an effort to give this problem a possible alternative viewpoint, is it at least feasible that the reason there are fewer black- and brown-colored Band-Aids conceivably due to some reason other than racism or bigotry?"
>
> **Lecturer**: "I cannot possibly see what else it would be. Do you have an alternative theory, sir?"
>
> **Me**: "Well, not a theory exactly. But I might venture, only because I'm in business school currently and learning about marketing and production concepts through a business lens – but I'm just wondering if maybe since there are fewer African-American and Mexican-American persons in this country (far fewer than the white people), could it be that population data may contribute to the use of fewer resources on items such as custom Band-Aids which would

exclusively serve a more niche community? Is that plausible, or do I have things way off?"

I sat down, genuinely curious. He paused for a moment and then spoke gruffly and loudly.

Lecturer: "Class, I want you to note long and hard what just happened here. I want you to notice how when a systemic and racist symptom of our culture is pointed out by a person of color, such as myself, it never fails for a white person (typically male) to stand up and defend the capitalistic hegemony. Oh, yes, they will always use the vernacular of the oppressor, which is to couch the language in 'business-focused' or 'rational' argumentation; but the end result is the same: the oppressor maintains dominance over the oppressed. Thank you, young man, for so vividly making my point. Let's continue…"

This is a true story. And while the exact phrasing is perhaps not 100% word-for-word, this happened, and it left me crushed.

I later retreated back to my dorm room and thought long and hard about my beliefs. *Was I racist?* Was I too white or too privileged to even see how racist I was? I closed my eyes and opened them again, revealing tears I didn't know were even forming. I don't know if they were tears of humiliation or introspection, but for some reason I was suddenly reminded of my moment on the red shag carpet floor in that church many years ago in nearby Burlington, Vermont. I felt bereft of joy. Cast out. *Faithless.*

Both memories still burn in my memory, and both are equally poignant.

Are these simply the cathartic mental bruises of a boy growing into adulthood? Possibly, so. And I'm sure every coming-of-age story in the world has a "this moment" or "that moment" which influences and guides the bearer's path forward. In my two cases, I felt the poignant sting when righteous belief shattered, and my faith faltered. It is not a pleasant feeling, nor is it always one to learn from. In most cases, these moments are just requisite to growing up and experiencing unsequestered life.

But in my case, it taught me a rare truth about religion and faith. Faith is deserved. It is earned. It should not be given out freely or flippantly. Faith is something that demands scrutiny and inspection. Counter to the later deviations of the word (as you'll read in the next chapter), I now believe faith is only viable when that which gives you faith stands up to reason and argumentation. Failing that, you have only empty words or a shadow-puppet of a deity with which to contend.

Truth stands up to criticism and inspection; truth stands up to guile and conceit. Truth stands up tall and rejoices in the light of the sun; it does not diminish or balk at critique. I choose to have *faith* in Truth. Whether that Truth is found in religion, science, ideology, or the spoken word, I choose to embrace it. I choose to debate with it ... to tease its secrets and push it violently for answers. Only then – only when it bathes freely in the light and begs for scrutiny, is it deserving of my reticent and unyielding **faith**.

FAITH (/FĀTH/). NOUN.

> ¹⁴Now fear the Lord and serve him with all faithfulness. Throw away the gods your ancestors worshiped beyond the Euphrates River and in Egypt and serve the Lord. ¹⁵ But if serving the Lord seems undesirable to you, then **choose for yourselves this day whom you will serve**, whether the gods your ancestors served beyond the Euphrates, or the gods of the Amorites, in whose land you are living.
>
> *Joshua 24:14-15*

F aith.

It is a curious word. The word "faith" first appeared in the 14th century. In ancient cultures, "faith" (like the Latin "fides") often referred to fidelity, loyalty, trust, or commitment without necessarily implying a lack of evidence; it was reliance on someone or something.

The etymology of the word "faith" is *Proto-Indo-European* (PIE) root *bheidh-*, which means roughly "confidence." The Latin word *fidēs* is derived from this root and means "trust." The word faith in English comes from the Anglo-French and Old French words *feid* and *feit*, which are ultimately derived from *fidēs*.

The more contemporary concepts of faith as *belief without evidence* became a focal point in discussions between religious believers and skeptics, where the latter argued that trust in something must be based on reason and evidence. They asserted that a belief in an idea should not be solely adhered to via the basis of blind acceptance, but rather should be supported by logical reasoning and verifiable facts.

Despite the arguments of the skeptics, "faith" as a complete trust in something, without proof, is almost universally considered a positive moniker in current society and its colloquial vernacular. The list of phrases and fortuitous idioms around one's faith are numerous.

- "Just try to *keep the faith*." *(generic)*
- "His faith in his friends was strong." *(faith in others)*
- "I have faith in the power of Jesus." *(religious faith)*
- "They never lost faith." *(generic)*
- "The organization acted in good faith." *(legal)*
- "She took a leap of faith!" *(spiritual)*

Without even knowing the full context, these are uplifting statements and constructive testaments to character, trust, or courage. It is considered inspiring to know someone *maintained their faith* in the face of hardship or adversity.

Conversely, not having faith is almost universally regarded with a negative connotation.

- "Sadly, they lost faith."
- "His faith abandoned him."
- "They acted in bad faith."
- "She just didn't have enough faith!"

In fact, to describe someone without faith, the word "faithless" was born. This rather doleful adjective imputes dishonesty. It means *disloyal, untrue, untrustworthy* or … *unfaithful*. The word gained initial usage between 1250AD and 1300AD; the earliest known use of it in a written context was around 1390AD by the poet William Langland.

Conversely, "faithful" now means *truthful, correct, believable, authentic,* or *accurate.*

So then, "faithful" and "faithless" are antonyms which live on opposite ends of the "faith spectrum." On its face, that would seem to be the end of this semantic quagmire. However, there remains a far more pernicious form of faith: a *blind faith.*

Blind Faith

Linguistically speaking, having a "blind" faith in something is universally negative. The phrase emerged in the early 1500s, with the earliest recorded usage found in the writings of Thomas More. The term "blind faith" is understood to be dangerous and invariably leads to poor decisions or actions. Examples abound:

"She put her money and faith blindly in the new investment scheme."

"Their faith was blind; it led them off a cliff."

"The politician's supporters showed blind faith in him."

"Blind faith in the cult leader had them soon drinking poison."

But now we come to the point. I ask you this: is not all religious faith "blind" at its roots?

The very nature of religion is to believe in the unseen. To believe in something which cannot be empirically proven or showcased. It is one's faith in something unseen that gives it its power—and similarly imbues that faith with any real meaning.

Hebrews 11:1 reads: "*Now faith is the assurance of things hoped for, the conviction of things not seen.*"

2 Corinthians 5:7 goes on to say: "*For we walk by faith, not by sight.*"

John 20:29: "*Jesus said to him, 'Have you believed because you have seen me? Blessed are those who have not seen and yet have believed.'*"

Is such pure faith not, by its very definition, **blind**? For the things that are seeable—knowable—don't require faith. They simply are. But faith is reserved for the rare things that must be believed without seeing—*without knowing*.

So, then, if not by unseeing, what then makes someone's faith "blind?" For if being without faith is undesirable, what makes faith in something disagreeable or distressing? Unless it is stated *ex post facto*, is not the "blind" qualifier appended onto someone *else's* faith by another only when they are *faithless* or unbelieving of that which gives the other his faith?

By way of an example, consider the sentence: "Poor boy; he has such blind faith in her!"

The meaning is immediately clear to anyone who reads it. But when we attempt to further dissect the meaning from the words themselves, things get messy. Looking closely, the subtext of the preceding sentence is all balled-up in the two-word idiom: "blind faith."

Is the boy's faith in another person (seemingly a lover in this context) negative? Why? Because it is blind. But how is/was it blind? Seemingly (per the insinuation) she was *faithless* and cheated on him (or the implication is she *may* cheat or *will* cheat).

So simply by placing the word "blind" as the modifier of "faith," the speaker has implicitly posited, *prima facie*, that the boy's faith in the object of his faith (the girl) is misplaced.

But that implication is imposed by a *third party*; it is not certain or known. It is hardly empirical.

In fact, the reader/listener is taking it completely "on faith" that the speaker knows what they're talking about. Unless there is specific evidence of impropriety by the girl, there is no way to know if the faith of the boy in the girl is truly "blind" (read: misplaced) or if it is the 'good' form of faith worth hanging on to.

To take this linguistic rathole one step further, another person might impart wisdom on the boy who reads the earlier quote, by affirming him: "Keep your faith and ignore the naysayers; your faith in her will be rewarded."

Faith is a Currency

Hence, it should be clear: faith is a subjective beast—or, at least, a form of currency to be spent wisely or unwisely. It is *blind* only when it is misspent on the "wrong" persons or ideas (which are completely subjective and only known in hindsight). And faith is *kept* or is *good* when it is spent on the "right" ideas or persons (also completely subjective and only known in hindsight).

Ergo, faith is completely idiosyncratic. And in an evolving world where subjectivity is now practically seen as divine, faith is the cardinal coin to save or frivolously spend!

I bring all this up in the holistic, cultural context of "misspent" faith. Because in this current era of rampant

Postmodernism, one person's truth is another person's lie. One's heretic is another's hero. One's fascist is another's saint. One's terrorist is another's freedom fighter. And one's *Right* is another's *Wrong*.

But what matters most of all to the faith peddler is that the gilded coin of faith be spent—indiscriminately if needed, but spent, nonetheless.

It is human nature to seek significance through faith. It is part of our "chemical makeup." We need to believe … to believe in something—*anything*. We require a belief structure. We deeply yearn for something bigger and better than ourselves. We recognize our own limitations—either as individuals, or as a species. Authors far smarter than myself, including my own brother, have written a lot about this topic and accurately describe it as "the meaning crises." The human soul craves meaning; absent God, it will fill the void of meaning with whatever it finds—even if the object of that craving is limited or deeply flawed. Faith is the conduit to finding and holding onto some form of meaning.

Without faith, we falter. We dissolve into fear and doubt. We descend low and feel incomplete. Without faith, we are perhaps not truly human. That is a curious statement, but I believe it to be completely true. Said another way, human beings have a faith-sized hole in our "heart" (for lack of a better term). We desperately thirst for some form of an identifying ideology that defines who we are and how we should view the world around us. It is faith that allows us to attain purpose by seeking after the essence of meaning.

For many people, that faith is religious in nature. Since perhaps the dawn of recorded history, man has relied on religious faith to guide his morality, perspectives, culture, habits, beliefs, and behavior. His faith was in God/gods and with it the religious text(s) that explained or guided his relationship with or to God(s). This was the *status mundi* ("state of the world") for global society's connection with meaning for most of recorded history.

Today we simply face a different face of God—a new religion. As Nietzsche famously said, "God is dead. God remains dead. And we have killed him." But I vehemently disagree. God is not dead! Nor does he remain dead. The God our soul craves – the faith-worshiping figure our soul sings out to – has not died, but simply morphed. Many have given Him a new face, a new altar, a new heaven, a new hell, and a new name. But their collective faith and search for meaning is as strong as ever!

A Woke God

For many, the god of today is a god of Wokeism! This god still demands prayer and supplication; she still requires sacrifice. And like the gods of old she, too, requires that the coin of faith be spent on her mercurial will.

For all the best virtues and worst vices of religion continue to lay bare upon her mighty altar. The religious zealotry is exercised tenfold; the idolatry to the Woke God is just as robust as it was for Ra, Jehovah, Baal, or Zeus. The deadly bifurcation separating the "believers" from the "unfaithful" is as exercised as ever. The god of today is alive and well-worshipped; religious faith perseveres! Worship songs are sung, and tributes are given. The language of her Church is preached in lecture halls by the ideologically pure. The vernacular used in the homilies, sermons, and seminars has simply changed from a focus on merciful grace to *social justice*—from heaven and hell to *equality* and *oppression*.

Thus, this reformed Postmodern culture has shifted away from a deity-based religious faith to a new religion: a woke-based religious faith. Whether or not this change is a good one remains to be seen. But let us not too quickly offer up the modifier "blind" to the faith of the reverent acolytes just yet. To be completely fair, one must apply the same yardstick to all religious dogmas.

The Third Rails: Religion & Politics

It is not lost on this writer that faith-based discussions often land on "deaf ears" (or perhaps to keep the analogy I will say "blind eyes"). There is a reason why wise folks attest that in polite company it's never a good idea to bring up either religion or politics. Why? The very reason these ideologies are so emotionally sensitive is because they are so closely linked to one's **personal identity** and their *faith*.

If you were to argue with someone about the weather or the price of gasoline, these are objective facts that can be easily researched and clarified. Not so with religion or politics! These are metaphysical and philosophical topics that are richly imbued with deep *meaning*. As such, they carry a greater order of *hierarchical complexity* than other subjects. They are what life is all about; so, naturally, it is common knowledge to completely ignore such topics in polite company.

If your brother believes that it rained last Tuesday, yet you are quite certain it was sunny, then a simple search for the facts will reveal the truth. If the weather record revealed rain, you would likely apologize with a smirk and give your brother credit for having the better memory. Similarly, if evidence proved the weather was sunny, your brother would be just as likely to concede the point with no ill will.

Yet, if the conversation was to move to a faith-based subject such as religion, the situation changes immeasurably. Even if the argument was on a completely verifiable topic, there likely is no evidence one brother might reveal that will convince the other brother to concede the point.

The Faith/Identity Entanglement Problem

One primary reason for this phenomenon is the *Entanglement Problem* between one's identity and their faith(s). A man's faith in his core beliefs is incorruptible in his eyes and thus sacrosanct. One's faith is part of who they are! It defines them. It *is* them.

Another's *wrong* opinion or reasoned argument should not shatter your pure faith. If you lose your faith, you lose your identity; if that happens then who are you, really? You are a person without an identity—a person without faith. And most would rather die than lose a crucial part of who they are; their identity is what sustains them and grounds them. So, they hold onto their faith with a savage ferocity and eschew all those who dare challenge their righteous faith. This is why even well-intentioned discussions quickly become debates and then fierce arguments. You are not having your *ideas* challenged; you're having your very *identity* attacked! It gets personal.

The Differing Value Systems Problem

The second reason why arguments involving religion or politics rarely achieve constructive outcomes is due to unequal yardsticks and differing value structures. For example, with the disagreement about the weather last Tuesday, it is easy to come to a resolution because there is a common and well-established baseline: a set of assumptions and shared values at play. The vernacular is also understood in advance; terms like "temperature" can be used and the definition of precipitation is understood by both parties. There are no differences in core values with respect to what weather is or what it is not.

If one brother understood the freezing point of water to be 32F and the other believed it to be "when I feel really cold," there would obviously be a misalignment and thus little opportunity for a reasoned discussion exists—at least until educational instruction was imparted and received.

Luckily this is not the case with most pragmatic topics. Ascertaining temperature or a specific precipitation is a straightforward exercise of empirical research. Indeed, probably the most controversial thing that could happen in such a debate would be finding that it was BOTH raining and sunny at the same time. And even in such a case, the facts would be met with bemusement and cordiality.

However, this is not so with faith-based topics. The yardsticks are, at best, individually defined and wildly subjective. And the value basis for discussions is often significantly different between two or more persons. You might spend 30 or 40 minutes discussing whether or not a particular Pope acted righteously in a certain situation, only to later find that your viewpoints on "righteousness" are diametrically opposed.

What is so interesting about such conversations is that the modality employed in conducting a faith-based conversation and an empirical conversation are extremely similar—on their face, at least. You can lay down all the "basics" at the beginning, agreeing along the way about timeline, historical events, familiar connections, even attributions of thought and emotions to certain actors. But as soon as the conversation swerves into the lane of *value constructs* or subjective reality, it will quickly veer off course. This, again, is largely because the faith-based yardsticks will not be the same size (or even employ the same metrics) between any two people on any value-based topic. Two people with opposing viewpoints will have a very hard time quantifying someone else's truth. It would be akin to one person trying to use the sensation of taste to explain to a blind person the color purple or for an engineer to try to use mathematical formulas to explain the brilliance of a rainbow to a child.

The Cognitive Bias Problem

The third reason why faith-based conversations "go off the rails" so quickly is perhaps the most important reason to grapple with and understand: *reduction* & *duality*. It is human nature to simplify complex, nuanced problems into smaller, manageable pieces that better fit into one's worldview. Faced with a lack of sufficient time (or data) to fully understand a topic, the human brain has great difficulty grappling with multi-layered complexity and nuance. So as a "coping" mechanism, it simplifies. It reduces a big problem into a far smaller and more manageable problem.

In short, the brain draws clear dividing lines separating black from white—even when the real situation is very "gray," or even a full spectrum of color! In this way, a bifurcation of **two** (2) opposing sides takes shape in the mind, even when the situation is far more complex—or *multiple* perspectives exist in reality. However, instead of BOTH sides being a little right—or both sides being entirely wrong—the brain forces one side to be comprised of cartoonish evil villains and the other side constituted as pure, unblemished angels.

The more troubling issue with this modality is how deep the poisoned well goes. With insufficient data to form a nuanced, multifaceted viewpoint, these 'black & white' opinions are formed quickly and then cemented in the brain to near permanent tribal-level beliefs, identity, and even memory itself. Thus, even when new data is later presented which contradicts the binary, self-prescribed, faith-based narrative, this evidence is outright rejected! Because, as stated above, such information contradicts the ideas now conflated with the person's identity.

What's so pernicious is how "sticky" these newly formed boolean viewpoints become. With little or no empirical data, an opinion is quickly formed positing that one of two *binary* options exist for a complex issue; this belief then permeates the conscious and subconscious. The insistence of binary truth (e.g. "this thing is good; that thing is bad") will endure in the belief structure even when additional information is later understood as true and verified.

This ability for the mind to quickly form stark opinions, and compartmentalize evidence that contradicts those opinions, is a phenomenon I first learned about in my undergraduate class *Psychology 101*. In one of the early chapters, the textbook explained that this "feature" (or is it a bug?) of the human brain causes prejudices and biases to form. Here is a short excerpt from the course material:

> "Bias can take many forms. You might be most familiar with bias in the context of prejudice or

discrimination against certain groups of people based on race, gender, or socioeconomic status. However, you can also be biased toward a certain idea or option. For example, confirmation bias can cause us to favor information that fits with our existing beliefs. This mental shortcut can lead [one] to overlook information that contradicts [their] preconceptions, like ignoring scientific research that disproves a health remedy [they] believe in.

While certain cognitive biases can help us make decisions more efficiently, it often hurts our ability to make decisions that are fair, rational, and favorable—for ourselves and everyone around us. The important thing to remember here is that humans will always hold bias. Since we can't really change how our brains work, learning to recognize bias in its various forms can help us become more aware of it and take steps to reduce negative consequences." (Warje)

This wisdom has stuck with me. I often catch myself reading a news story or listening to friends discuss a complex topic and feel a visceral desire to quickly form an opinion.

The Palestinians killed how many innocent people? They must be subhuman monsters!

Putin invaded an innocent country without being provoked? He must be a madman!

A gay, black man was attacked in downtown Chicago by Trump supporters? MAGA supporters must be racist and homophobic!

Without complete information, the mind desires resolution. It seeks a solution to a problem. It hungers for equilibrium. It is uncomfortable to live in a state of uncertainty—even for a short period of time. And our brains are not simple computers either; they are capable of millions (perhaps billions) of computations every second! But without sufficient information, the brain is frequently asked to make decisions quickly in order to take an action—such as *form an opinion*. This process is not a trivial exercise.

As a species, we are social creatures, of course. And part of living in a society is forming opinions that allow us to fit in and respond to situations as a group. So, opinion-formation is a critical action that the brain is asked to do over and over again—and usually with only a limited amount of data. As a coping (read: defensive) mechanism, the brain forms biases and rushes to sort through complex information quickly.

Perhaps this is a modern miracle of evolution. Think of the alternative: *with limited information, the brain shuts down and cannot form thoughts or opinions until further information is provided.* If our brains worked like this, it's likely that protohumans never would have made it out of their caves. Biases towards new (unknown) foods allowed us to avoid being poisoned. Biases towards new (unknown) people allowed us to avoid being killed. These biases and prejudices are defensive in our cultural evolution for a reason. Our species is tribal. When a new tribe entered the area, it was wise to fear and loathe them on sight. If we were overly trusting, we likely would have had our food and shelter stolen.

Perhaps man is right to be immediately defensive (and even a tad barbaric) at times. Think of our past. To summarize the history of our species, a group fights to take control and gain dominance over its peers. Then others step in and take dominance over that group. Man has lied, stolen, cheated, plotted, raped, tortured, and killed to gain superiority over other men. It is no mystery that "stranger danger" has worked itself into our lizard brains and become permanently ingrained into our amygdala. Bias is evolutionarily sound and justified.

That all said, the question becomes: "what, if anything, can we do to prevent *unhealthy* bias?" Can we put our lizard brains on hold in a contemporary sense and seek to process information rationally and logically? Yes, I think so. But it isn't painless; and it certainly isn't "normal." Because a simple, **false** story is infinitely easier for our brains to process than a complex, **true** one. But with enough militant *faith*, many believe they can coerce the simple story to be true.

"Normal" Thinking

Normality is binary thinking. It's reacting quickly to situations and subconsciously processing information into two distinct camps—just as our brain has been programed to do over millions of years of evolution. Normality is to hate quickly, empathize little, and put logical reasoning on hold. Normality is to go with the flow and give into *groupthink*. Normality is focused on *survival,* as opposed to *living* and enriching the world around us. Normality is easy. "Complex thinking" is difficult and takes work. And people, on the whole, hate to work.

"We can at least try to understand our own motives, passions, and prejudices, so as to be conscious of what we are doing when we appeal to those of others. This is very difficult, because our own prejudice and emotional bias always seems to us so rational."
— T. S. Eliot, The Aims of Education

It is so easy and "normal" to analyze a situation and then with limited (or no) information, immediately bifurcate it into binary viewpoints. Cementing this axiom, our emotions are easy to manipulate and used to further drain out the monochromatic blacks and whites from an otherwise diverse color spectrum. Given a situation that is nuanced, complex, and multi-faceted, nothing cuts through to "the heart of the matter" (or so we tell ourselves) like *emotional appeal*. This is why propaganda and emotionally charged slogans work so well!

For example, in the case of the draft during the Vietnam War: the conversation wasn't around the nuances of forced labor and conscription, but instead became all about "national pride" and "signing up to serve your country." Those who chose to disobey the demand for compulsory enlistment quickly became "draft dodgers," "unpatriotic," and even "enemies to their country."

Bifurcation is easiest when emotion can be used to aid in propaganda.

In the case of whether to mandate a Covid-19 vaccine circa 2021, the national conversation for the decision centered not around bodily autonomy, tyrannical government control, efficacy concerns, or resultant injuries due to prematurely rushing a vaccine's release; rather, the emotionally charged narrative centered around pithy one-liners such as "killing grandma," "following the guidelines," "being in this together," "trusting the Science™" and "doing your part."

The ability for humans to fit complex topics into neat-and-tidy packages is a "feature" (not a bug) of evolution. What is a bug, however, is the inability to process new information after it's available and use it to amend the original programming. And the most significant problem with this paradigm is that once the dividing lines are drawn, they are rarely erased. The other side becomes the literal devil; and "your side" consists entirely of virtue paragons.

Sadly, no amount of evidence to the contrary will allow a person who has formed a cognitive bias to fully understand the multifaceted complexities once they've convinced themselves the matter is binary; their brain has turned off the ability to see the diverse rainbow of colors in the palette. There is only white and black—only good and bad; only evil and righteousness exists. All "middle ground" goes out the window and fades away— all because the brain is defensive of its identity and its faith-based opinions.

What is sadder still is that the more important the subject, the more fiercely the human mind will defend its limited and myopic viewpoint. Once the Capulets and the Montagues start feuding, there is very little to be said to convince one who has taken sides to see it from the other's perspective; as such, little headway can be made to stop the bloodshed. One who advocates for 'Team Black' cannot cognitively see White's perspective, and one who is on 'Team White' cannot cognitively put themselves in Black's shoes. Forced, and even violent, duality of perspective is perhaps the human condition.

It is then no real irony that we have divided our own human races into groupings based on literal color. We quite consciously choose to pit "blacks" or "browns" against "whites." Bizarrely, instead of ameliorating these divides and seeking a salve for the wounds, Postmodern society—with brazen, *woke*, spiritual fervor—chooses to fan the flames of racial tensions and hyper-focus on what *separates us* vs what makes us the same. As such, the Woke God willingly chooses to bifurcate the world by skin color, not because she should, but because she can. And our lizard brains tend to win out every time against reason, logic, truth, and reality. Why? Because humanity feeds on turmoil and blind faith. Our faith in our own biases – no matter how impure or how empirically inaccurate, guides our path.

The Golden Idol

As mentioned, faith is a precious currency that demands to be spent. Man seeks for God but resurrects idols instead. He thirsts for meaning, but instead chokes down lies spread by charlatans. In either case, we mortal men and women consume faith like fire consumes oxygen. We ferociously devour the promises that faith and allegiance to a god avows. We require it to sustain our souls. Submerged below the waves of uncertainty, faith is a paper straw we use to desperately suck air into our lungs. It is a reflex action for our breathing soul; we can no more turn off our need to spend the coin of faith than we can choose to cease breathing. Unfortunately, the *object* of our faith seems almost inconsequential compared to the desire to spend our faith.

Like a drug addict, mankind desperately seeks a high; the drug itself to get us there is unimportant. This is why when Moses descended from Mount Sinai after communing with the Supreme Being and brought down the commandments of God manifest on rock tablets, he found when he returned not a pious and reflecting people hungry for the fruits of the Lord—but rather a people driven mad without a proper outlet for their righteous faith. They had grown so inpatient waiting for Truth they sought to satiate themselves with a golden idol: a self-made, physical manifestation of their meaning crisis.

They rejected God to instead employ a blind faith *vis-a-vis* a cheap manifestation of God.

Their *faith* was what mattered most—far more than Truth. Leaderless, their faith persisted and demanded release, like an insatiable itch to be scratched or a throbbing, sexual desire. Absent a physical vessel in which to direct their faith, the Israelites erected their own: a golden calf. If the story of Exodus is to be believed, this was a people who had JUST exited Egypt—after no fewer than ten plagues were laid upon the land by God Himself. This was a people who had just seen the Red Sea part by the hand of God as they escaped oppression and slavery. This was a people whose faith would expectedly be *visceral* and *strong*. Nevertheless, in the absence of religious leadership, the curse of human weakness had them abandon the object of their faith and quickly take up another. For the laws of faith are perhaps like the laws of energy – it cannot be created or destroyed, just *transformed* into another shape or directed at another object.

In the case of the Israelites, in the space of around forty days, their faith transformed from faith in Yahweh to a faith in an idol made of gold. As transcribed in the Bible: "[This calf] **is** thy gods, O Israel, which have brought thee up out of the land of Egypt." (Exodus 32:8) *[emphasis added]*.

In other words, fearing Moses would not return, the Israelites lost no time declaring the golden calf to BE their God—the very God that delivered them from Egypt a few weeks earlier. Their faith didn't leave them; it just mutated and then transfixed into a physical form. The idol was present; Moses was not. The golden calf could be felt; God could not.

Metamorphosis of Faith

Our current Postmodern culture now finds itself facing a similar crisis of faith—or at least a *metamorphosis of faith*. The faith in our religious institutions and our past God(s) are crumbling. But the *faith void* does not stay empty for long.

Faith in a new *Church of Wokeism* has been taking shape since 2014 and quickly gaining ardent disciples. It is a new religion, so its aims are still developing, and its tomes still being written. But just like the religions of old, this new religion requires awesome faith, devotion, supplication, obedience, and conformance to the wills of a jealous and capricious god. This new religion of Wokeism thirsts for golden coins of faith—and demands that they be spent with fevered abundance. They are to be melted down and turned into a great and glorious new idol to worship.

Our immortal souls thirst bitterly for truth and for meaning – and religious faith is the conduit for such divine desires. The soul's need for faith cannot and shall not be denied. But is prayerful faith in the Woke God one that best serves mankind, or preys on it?

Let us explore that question together...

WHAT IS WOKE?

It is probably a good time to define terms. For one person's trash is another person's treasure. So, I will attempt to be precise with language in an attempt to add maximum clarity.

Woke History

But first, let's dive into a bit of history. The term "Woke" maintains its roots in Black culture; initially it was used as a derivative form of "awake," with phrases such as "stay woke" to mean "stay awake" or "pay attention" (specifically, to a sensitive issue involving Black discrimination). The word has been used as far back as the 1940s. The first recorded instance of the word was by a Black union leader in a strike against discriminatory pay; the pamphlet read *"We were asleep. But we will **stay woke** from now on."*

Up until the mid-2010s, the word was used sparsely and almost exclusively by the African American community. In 2014, the word faced the public and political arena in a significant way following the death of Michael Brown in Ferguson, Missouri. This situation sparked the Black Lives Matter (BLM) movement.

Origins and Timeline of the Word Woke

1923
In 1923, a collection of aphorisms and ideas by the Jamaican philosopher and social activist Marcus Garvey included the summons, **"Wake up Ethiopia! Wake up Africa!"**

1940
The Negro United Mine Workers launch a strike in West Virginia against discriminatory pay. A Black union leader speaks about learning they were being paid less than their white counterparts, "we were asleep. But we will **stay woke** from now on."

1962
William Melvin Kelley's essay **"If You're Woke, You Dig It"** appears in the *New York Times*.

1938
Blues musician Huddie Ledbetter, known as Lead Belly, uses the phrase **"stay woke"** in his song "Scottsboro Boys."

1972
Author Barry Beckham uses the word **"woke"** in his 1972 play *Garvey Lives!*

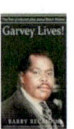

The moniker "Woke" soon became intertwined with the BLM movement; as it grew, so did the word. It had a dual meaning; it signaled awareness of injustice or racial tension, but also became a word of action. Activists were *Woke* and called on sympathizers to their cause to "stay woke."

In 2017 the word *Woke* was added to the Oxford English Dictionary—defined as "being 'aware' or 'well-informed' in a political or cultural sense."

2008
Erykah Badu's 2008 song "Master Teacher" uses the lyrics **"stay woke."**

2017
Appearance of **"Stay Woke"** as a category on *Jeopardy!*

2022
Florida Gov. Ron Desantis signs into law, "Stop W.O.K.E."

2010s
Woke undergoes dilution and starts being used broadly as a catch-all to describe social justice—it quickly becomes appropriated and transformed into a negative descriptor for anything having to do with inclusivity and anti-discrimination.

2020
Hulu comedy series *Woke* premieres.

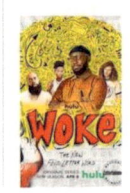

However, in the early 2020s a major metamorphosis happened for the word *Woke* as its meaning began to violently shift—and then, before you knew it, was *entirely co-opted* by white liberal progressives. Nearly overnight, the 'Woke' ceased being a word to empower Black activism.

Progressive-leaning *Wikipedia* cites the evolution of the word under the section "2015–2019: Broadening Usage" of its article on "Woke." It states:

> "While the term woke initially pertained to issues of racial prejudice and discrimination impacting African Americans, it came to be used by other activist groups with *different causes*. [3] While there is no single agreed-upon definition of the term, it came to be primarily associated with ideas that involve identity and race and which are promoted by progressives, such as the notion of *white privilege* or *slavery reparations* for African Americans […]
>
> The term has gained popularity amid an increasing leftward turn on various issues among the American Left; this has partly been a reaction to the right-wing politics of U.S. President Donald Trump, who was elected in 2016, but also to a growing awareness regarding the extent of historical discrimination faced by African Americans. [31] According to Perry Bacon Jr., ideas that have come to be associated with 'wokeness' include a *rejection of American exceptionalism*; a belief that the *United States has never been a true democracy*; that *people of color suffer from systemic and institutional racism*; that *white Americans experience white privilege*; that *African Americans deserve reparations for slavery* and post-enslavement discrimination; that disparities among racial groups, for instance in certain

professions or industries, are *automatic evidence of discrimination*; that U.S. law enforcement agencies are designed to discriminate against people of color and so should be defunded, disbanded, or heavily reformed ['*Defund the Police*']; that *women suffer from systemic sexism*; that *individuals should be able to identify with any gender or none*; that *U.S. capitalism is deeply flawed*; and that Trump's election to the presidency was not an aberration but a reflection of the prejudices about people of color held by large parts of the U.S. population. [31]"

Woke Stolen from the Black Community

To summarize, the term "Woke" – which existed since the 1940s as a symbol of power and resistance uniquely for the Black oppression movement – in very short order was completely misappropriated to represent such a *litany* of Progressive issues that the word lost its original meaning.

What is particularly ironic about the co-opting of the historically Black-owned word "Woke," is that its theft was largely by *white* Progressives on the Left. While decrying themselves advocates of the African Americans with whom they allied, this historically Black word and the phraseology around it, imbued in black culture, was completely debased and stolen from them. In the most insidious way possible, advocacy groups (run primarily by white persons) poached and reappropriated the word "Woke" to such a degree that it is now almost meaningless. It most certainly no longer means "stay awake" (to Black discrimination). Rather, when the average person now hears the word 'Woke,' it is often associated with divisive or ideological arguments embroiled in gender/transgender rights, power hierarchies, DEI programs, or even suggestions like putting tampons in men's bathrooms.

To use a British idiom, the Progressive Left "took the piss out of the whole thing." And, sadly, black advocates for Black causes sat back and let it happen under their noses.

This isn't entirely their fault, mind you. The Progressive Left has a way of turning up the temperature dial ever, ever so slowly as the frog sits in the pot that he doesn't even know he's being boiled alive. For this essentially is what happened to Black America when White Progressives came in, usurped their language, promised them meaningful change, bled the word *Woke* dry of all meaning, and then moved onto their next crusade.

Because it wasn't quite enough to have this country steal Africans from their home, drag them to America, force them into slavery, impose Jim Crow on them after they were freed, and marginalize them for 250 years; now the Progressive Left throws a dash of salt into their wounds by co-opting part of their language under a feigned banner of partnership.

Beyond the irony of the situation, the pilfered word 'woke' has become so overused (and abused) that it now means almost anything to anyone who chooses to use it (for good or for bad). Yes, it means fighting against *injustice* (as it always did), but no longer exclusively *Black injustice*. Now, its meaning is like a week-old Jambalaya – with a little bit of everything thrown in a jumbled, Progressive soup! It means socialism. It means anti-fascism. It means pro-democracy and anti-capitalism. It means trans rights. And women's rights. And gay rights. And certainly, above all, it means anti-Trump!

Woke now deigns to mean a hodgepodge of Progressive ideologies so vast that the poor term struggles to keep up with its towering aims. For even if you *agree* with all the Progressive Left's goals and principles, it is not healthy (nor possible) for a single moniker to carry such weight. The word soon falters and buckles under the strain of too heavy a load. And when a word is so overused (and so misused) to mean everything to everyone, it becomes nothing to no one; it lays down in a heap, worthless and counter-purpose to the goals of the group trying to use it.

In short, *Woke* now means "everything I like" to the Progressive Left. Conversely, on the other side of the duopoly, it now means "everything I hate" to the Right.

Shifting Meaning of Words

Bill Marr summarized the situation fairly well in an interview on CNN:

> "The Democrats can sometimes take it too far—I would categorize 'liberal' as different from 'woke'. You know, 'woke' which started out as a good thing – 'alert to injustice' – who could be against that? But it became sort of an eyeroll because they love diversity except of ... *ideas*! And that's not really where we should be. I mean, they have a trail of VERY bad ideas. Woke ideas."

Jake Tapper then asks him to define *Wokeness,* and Marr responds:

> "Well, again, I think it's [now] this *collection of ideas* that are not building on liberalism, but very often undoing it. I mean, five years ago Abraham Lincoln was not a controversial figure of the liberals. We liked him (*haha*). Now they take his name off schools and tear down his statues. Really, Lincoln isn't good enough for you? Five, ten years ago bedroom liberalism was striving to be a **color-blind society**:

'we don't see race' (of course we see it, but it doesn't matter.) That's not what 'woke' is! Woke is something very different. It's identity politics; we see it all the time … it's always the most important thing. I don't think that's liberalism."

Words shifting in their meaning over time is hardly new. In fact, as any linguist will tell you, it's par for the course. 'Linguistic Irony' is a form of irony where a word or phrase can morph over time to literally mean the exact opposite of its intended definition. Examples of words that have significantly shifted in meaning include:

- "awful" (originally meaning "inspiring awe" now meaning "very bad"),
- "literally" (once exclusively meant literally, now also means "figuratively")
- "nice" (once meant "foolish," now means "pleasant"),
- "terrible" (originally signifying "inspiring terror," now means "extremely bad"),
- "silly" (once meant "blessed," now means "foolish"),
- "bully" (historically meant "sweetheart," now refers to someone who intimidates others),
- "egregious" (originally meant "outstanding," now means "flagrantly bad"), and
- "villain" (historically referred to a peasant or serf in feudal society, now used to describe an evil character)
- "cloud" (derived from a word meaning "rock" or "mountain" in Old English)

We can now add "woke" to the list of unhappy words which were changed, morphed, or "abused" to such an extent that they now mean in English the exact opposite of their original intent.

Obsessed with identity politics, *Woke* is now undergoing an *existential identity crisis*. Since the term *Woke* is confused and means so many things to so many people, it now means less than nothing. The Right sees Wokeism as its *mortal enemy*. The Left sees it as its stalwart champion of social justice. A binary has formed!

But a simple word cannot live in a vast cultural canyon for very long. It cannot be so pregnant with meaning and describe so much to BOTH sides that it survives. The Right has (perhaps rightly, perhaps wrongly) made *Woke* its villain; those championing "Stay Woke" are cartoonish devils. On the other hand, the Left has made Wokeness its beacon of light and a righteous banner to triumphantly march behind; those who profane those *Staying Woke* are cliché devils – deserving of labels such as "Hitler," "fascist," "bigot" (and surely are pot-marked in "phobias" galore)!

The two sides have fallen victim to *Binary Thinking* and *Confirmation Bias* described in the previous chapter. Instead of listening to each other's perspectives, dividing lines are drawn, pitchforks seized, and war drums banged. The Capulets and the Montagues will never find peace when both sides cling to mind-numbing words and banners to make their arguments for them.

For there to be a *balm in Gilead*, critical thinking and nuanced discussion is required around multifaceted issues. Few issues are binary—especially the faith-based ones. So, it is imperative we begin to move away from assigning single words or monochromatic perspectives to complex issues in vain attempts to make them all neat and tidy...

LEFT: "I'm woke, you're not. End of story. Don't talk to me, racist!"

RIGHT: "You're inflicted with the *woke mind virus*. I can't listen to anything you say!"

These are dividing lines and bifurcation points. They are unhelpful. Precise words with actual meaning should form entire sentences and then paragraphs and then discussions—which in turn should form coherent thoughts and foster real debate. These should be our weapons, not monochromatic terms that are as empty as they are unsophisticated.

Sermon Recap

So, what is *Woke*? Well, the moniker means so many different things to many different groups of people. Because of this fact, the word "woke" is a divisive word, devoid of any real substance.

What humanity deserves is a rainbow of vibrant language pregnant with nuance and meaning. We need introspective *discussions* about sensitive issues and complex topics. When we retreat behind a single word to say "everything," we wind up saying nothing at all.

Words are tools. And the word "woke" is a broken and busted tool—it's sadly been all worn out by Progressive ideologues who vainly attempted in their hubris to use one single word on too many applications. They have whipped that poor horse to a sad and agonizing death! And the Right is just as myopic, choosing to malign that same word and decry it with every ounce of impugnation they can impose.

Therefore, "Woke" is linguistically broken; it exhausted its purpose and now deserves to live in the dustbin of

Postmodern history. Instead, we must take up and sharpen our instruments of language; we must use them to erect bridges and foster greater understanding between a people divided.

Complex ideas require complex tools. Language is one such valuable tool. Let's sharpen and use *precise* words, phrases, and complex levels of discourse that rebuild this world instead of using monosyllabic, schismatic words that tear our American family into two distinct, belligerent encampments.

Is this possible?

Yes!

I shall explain exactly how in the chapters to follow…

"The masses are never right."
— *Oscar Wilde*

DIALECTIC BREAKDOWN & FORMING SYNTHESIS

Hegelian dialectics (or the *dialectic method*) essentially is an introspective dialogue (or debate) between persons or groups holding differing points of view about a subject but wishing to arrive at the truth through reasoned argumentation.

For the purpose of literary deconstruction, I will use the dialectic process—and specifically the concepts of *thesis* and *antithesis* to come together and form a *dialectical synthesis*—which in theory is a whole greater than the sum of its parts.

Via this method we can analyze the Woke paradigm with the aim of coming to a rational assessment of its value to society. Now, to be fair, "rational" is itself a subjective term when viewed through the deconstructive Postmodern framework; but let's put that aside for a moment knowing it will be factored into the following argumentation.

For a constructive understanding of the term Wokeism, it is critical to understand it as the product of the Postmodern era of ideas and suppositions, which is inherently a deconstructive framework.

Eras (or "cultural epochs") represent segments of time where the cultural totality of the combined human rationality—while consistently changing and undergoing metamorphosis—demonstrates certain pervasive themes. The most contemporary cultural epochs are as follows:

Pre-Modernity→ Modernity → Postmodernism → Metamodernism

Pre-Modernity

The period of Pre-Modernity generally refers to the historical period before the start of Modernity (aka "The Modern Era"), which is usually considered to begin around the 15th century with inventions like the printing press and the Age of Exploration. In other words, the Pre-Modern era encompasses most of the Medieval period and earlier times, with the exact dates varying depending on the region and historical context—essentially, the time before the Enlightenment and significant industrialization.

Pre-Modernity is characterized by agrarian societies with low technological development, strong community ties based on tradition and ascribed status, limited social mobility, a reliance on religious authority, and a worldview deeply rooted in religious adherence and ritual. Moreover, this period is specifically known for humanity at large finding meaning through faith in God, typically via organized religion.

Modernity

The epoch of Modernity was characterized by belief in progress, reason, and individual autonomy. It is further broken down into sub classifications of "Early Modernity" (roughly 1500-1789), "Classical Modernity" (1789-1900), and "Late Modernity" (1900-1989). The core values associated with Modernity include individualism, rationalism, scientific progress, secularism, democracy, urbanization, technological innovation, and a belief in individual rights and freedoms, often manifested through the rise of the nation-state and capitalist economic systems.

Postmodernism

The cultural epoch of Postmodernism is a reaction against the certainties of Modernity—embracing irony, skepticism, and the idea that there are no absolute truths. This epoch roughly stretches from the 1950s through the end of the 20th century (and maintains a heavy influence on the present era as well). It is a period of *deconstructionism*, where established paradigms are flipped on their head and "sacred cows" are slaughtered. Although stated in 1882, Friedrich Nietzsche's iconic asseveration "God is dead [...] and we have killed him" epitomizes this era, as society sought to cast off all vestiges of absolute truth posited by religion. Today, most scholars argue that humanity is not fully in the era of Postmodernism anymore, but its influence is still extremely present in contemporary culture—insinuating we are likely living in a "post-Postmodern" era where many aspects of

Postmodernism remain relevant, but new ideas are emerging to take its place.

Metamodernism

This leads us to the current era. The burgeoning epoch of the present bears the moniker "Metamodernism." Perhaps beginning as soon as the early 2000s, this "beyond Postmodernism" phase strives to reconcile the so-called optimism and certainty of Modernity with the critical awareness of Postmodernity—often oscillating between hope and irony.

Whereas Modernity was concerned with ideas of classification, stratification, and construction—namely seeking for meaning through emergence—Postmodernism primarily is "addition through subtraction" and purely deconstructionist. Obsessively concerned with critique, it does not make its own assessments of truth, but rather seeks to undermine, criticize, and lambast the so-called veracities that have become ingrained in society outcropping from Modernity.

To determine if Metamodernism dialectically synthesizes Modernity and Postmodernism, we want to look at some quintessential examples from the Postmodern era. Can we examine the postmodern framework of Wokeism to determine and evaluate the emergence of *synthesis*?

Postmodernism's Architype

I assert that *Wokeism* is Postmodernism's pivotal architype. To evaluate this claim, let's consider 21st century Wokeism as the totality of the concepts, tautologies, precepts, values, and collective wisdom that the Woke ideology espouses (taking, for granted, that its meaning has considerably shifted over a relatively short period of time). Steel-manning its positive benefit, the *thesis* statement then would be:

> *"Wokeism has benefited society at large by allowing a greater awareness of discrimination and injustice by its ability to highlight areas where gross power dynamics subvert or relegate those with less power. The goal of this awareness ('waking up') is galvanization of the culture into action and pushing for significant changes to resolve these power imbalances."*

The *antithesis* for this argumentation might be stated by a member of the "Anti Woke" encampment, as follows:

> *"Wokeism prioritizes subjective lived experiences and social narratives over objective reality and empirical evidence, which can undermine constructive problem-solving. This approach risks distorting facts to fit ideological goals, leading to policies and cultural shifts disconnected from practical or measurable outcomes. The undue focus on identity and ideological conformity over merit and open dialogue stifles free speech and creates division."*

We are faced with a bit of a challenge with these stated *thesis* and *antithesis* statements. The most significant problem, and a critique of Wokeism, is its vast umbrella across so many different areas of cultural concern. We might focus on multiple areas or substrates of Wokeism. I'll cite only a couple specific examples from across the rather broad "Woke Spectrum." I invite other authors to continue this thought experiment and analyze it further.

Dialectical Synthesis (Gender Example)

In general, Modernity took it for granted that gender was binary (male and female). This conclusion relied on constructs such as biology, cultural norms, and other observable biological evidence such as chromosomal patterns (XX and XY), reproductive anatomy, and secondary sexual characteristics. This perspective aligned with Enlightenment-era ideals of rationality, objectivity, and categorization, which sought to define and systematize human experience through empirical evidence and scientific inquiry. Gender was generally viewed as a natural and fixed extension of biological sex, reinforcing societal roles aligned with these binary categories.

The *Postmodern* ("Woke") viewpoint on transgenderism emphasizes the fluidity and socially constructed nature of gender, challenging the idea of fixed, binary categories tied strictly to biological sex. It prioritizes personal identity and subjective elements like "lived experiences," viewing gender as a self-determined and evolving concept shaped by cultural, historical, and individual contexts. Because, by definition, *Postmodernism* critiques traditional norms and power structures that enforce rigid gender roles, it naturally advocates for the recognition and validation of diverse gender identities and expressions.

A *Metamodern* perspective on transgenderism might seek to embrace the complexity of gender as an interplay between biology, culture, and personal experience, hoping to bridge *Modernist* reliance on scientific evidence with *Postmodernist* celebration of individual narratives. More importantly, a Metamodern viewpoint on the topic would reject polarized debates, advocating for an integrative approach that acknowledges biological realities and empirical practices that enhance well-being. Balancing empathy with pragmatism, Metamodernism would aim to foster inclusivity and societal cohesion, emphasizing the meaningfulness of individual identity journeys within a nuanced cultural context.

This may sound like a mouthful, but the breakdown is important. Specifically of note is the "journey" taken by humanity towards a positive outcome through a serpentine path of adversity, irrationality, and the absurd. I would be so bold as to use an analogy of a family's road trip: humanity needed to have the Postmodern "breakdown by the side of the road" in order to fully appreciate the ultimate destination once it is reached.

Metamorphosis

Postmodernism took the path of warring with Modernity so fiercely that it abandoned the empirical nature of biology itself. By virtue of choosing to view an objective element (such as binary gender) through a subjective lens, it demonstrated how far the pendulum could swing into the realm of the preposterous. But the *synthesis* of this irrational swing to the Left might ultimately turn a stationary and deformed chrysalis into a beautiful butterfly in the proliferating *Metamodern* era.

Consider the miracle of life. It is perhaps one of (if not THE) most precious and beautiful processes undergone by humans. Bringing new life into the world awakens hope, growth, and the evolution of our species. In this same way, the birthday of a new child is celebrated with awe, wonder, and sublime delight. However, consider at the same time the birthing pains of the woman who bestows that life to the world. It takes a profound level of pain, discomfort, and agony. The torture of childbirth is worth every second. It is *addition through subtraction*. The world is a far better place because it was able to work through the pain of the excruciating birthing experience.

The same is the case for the synthesis (Metamodernism) culminating from the dialectic process via convergence of the *thesis* (Postmodernism) and *antithesis* (Modernism). Postmodernism—complete with both its positives and excessive negatives—was necessary to bring about the cultural evolution we face in the current era.

In the case of Wokeism, humanity will likely find it needed to experience the spiritual rot of a profane new Religion just like the "pains of labor" was requisite in order to bring about a new and wonderful new cultural organism.

At all times society is growing, evolving, and *living*; for this reason, it is very much like a corporeal entity. We sometimes require great discomfort to experience rapture. The muscles of our body need to be tested (often painfully) to expand. Emerging out of reductive Postmodernism thought and into a new era of Metamodern philosophy will be a hard and difficult path. Mankind will continue to divide itself and create political schisms. The Left and Right will take up its pitchforks. Complex issues will be reduced to their lowest binary and monochromatic manifestations.

For Wokeism to be reborn requires a drastic, and perhaps violent, cultural and ideological shift. It will require evolution. It will require adaptation, rational thought, and logic. It will also require radical empathy. It will require *synthesis*.

THE HIERARCHY OF OPPRESSION

Since the early 1990s, many progressive authors have written on the topic of oppression (long before "Woke" was even a culturally significant term). To help provide a framework for determining the relative extent that different groups faced prejudice, the term *intersectionality* was coined by legal scholar Kimberlé Crenshaw in her 1989 paper *Demarginalizing the Intersection of Race and Sex: A Black Feminist Critique of Antidiscrimination Doctrine, Feminist Theory, and Antiracist Politics*. Crenshaw introduced the concept to describe how Black women face overlapping forms of discrimination that cannot be fully understood by considering racism and sexism independently:

> "The concept of intersectionality is not simply about the ways in which race and gender interact on multiple and often simultaneous levels, but also about the social and political institutions that reinforce these dynamics." (Crenshaw, 1989).

Ever since her seminal paper, intersectionality has been regarded as the primary framework used to examine how multiple forms of oppression—such as racism, sexism, classism, and homophobia—intersect and create unique experiences of marginalization for individuals who belong to multiple marginalized groups. It emphasizes that oppression is not experienced in isolation but is compounded and shaped by the overlapping identities and systems of power an individual navigates.

Postmodern frameworks (e.g. Wokeness) tend to reject rigid hierarchies of all types. Ergo, in theory it rejects a *Hierarchy of Oppression*, instead advocating for intersectional analysis that acknowledges compounded forms of disadvantage.

That said, there are certain heterodox texts within the *Book of Woke* that posit clear "hierarchies of oppression" in practice—although not always with any formality. This informal hierarchy is influenced by specific societal, cultural, and historical factors, as well as individual interpretations. Those near the top (most oppressed) receive the most favorable treatment by Woke media, thought leaders, academics, and ardent zealots in the *Church of Wokeism*.

The concept of *Woke* or "social justice" hierarchies often refers to a spectrum of marginalized or oppressed groups within society, based on historical and contemporary inequalities. This is subjective and varies depending on different perspectives, but generally, the hierarchy is based on *intersectionality*—i.e. how various forms of identity (race, gender, class, sexuality, ability, etc.) intersect and affect one's level of oppression.

Ranking Oppression

While this is not universally agreed upon, here is a rough outline of how some social justice movements and scholars might categorize groups based on their perceived levels of oppression, from most to least oppressed:

1. Transgender and Non-Binary People (especially trans women of color, who face high rates of violence, unemployment, and discrimination)
2. LGBTQ+ Persons (non-transgender or non-binary individuals within this group, especially people of color)
3. Black/African Americans (particularly Black women and LGBTQ+ individuals within this group)
4. Indigenous Peoples (Native Americans, First Nations, etc., who experience systemic disenfranchisement and erasure)
5. People with Disabilities (especially those who are also people of color or LGBTQ+)
6. Women (particularly women of color, disabled women, and women from lower socio-economic backgrounds)
7. People of Color (including Latinx, Asian Americans, etc., but not Black or Indigenous people who are listed separately due to the unique histories of oppression they face)
8. Immigrants/Refugees (especially undocumented individuals or those from war-torn or underprivileged regions)
9. Poor/Working-Class People (particularly those who are marginalized in other ways, such as race, gender, or disability)
10. Religious Minorities (e.g., Muslims, Jews, Sikhs, etc., especially in regions where they are systematically targeted)

HIERARCHY OF OPPRESSION

#1 TRANSGENDER
#2 LGBTQ+ (non-transgender)
#3 BLACK/AFRICAN AMERICANS
#4 INDIGENOUS PEOPLES
#5 PEOPLE WITH DISABILITIES
#6 WOMEN
#7 OTHER PERSONS OF COLOR (LATINX, ASIAN AMERICANS, ETC)

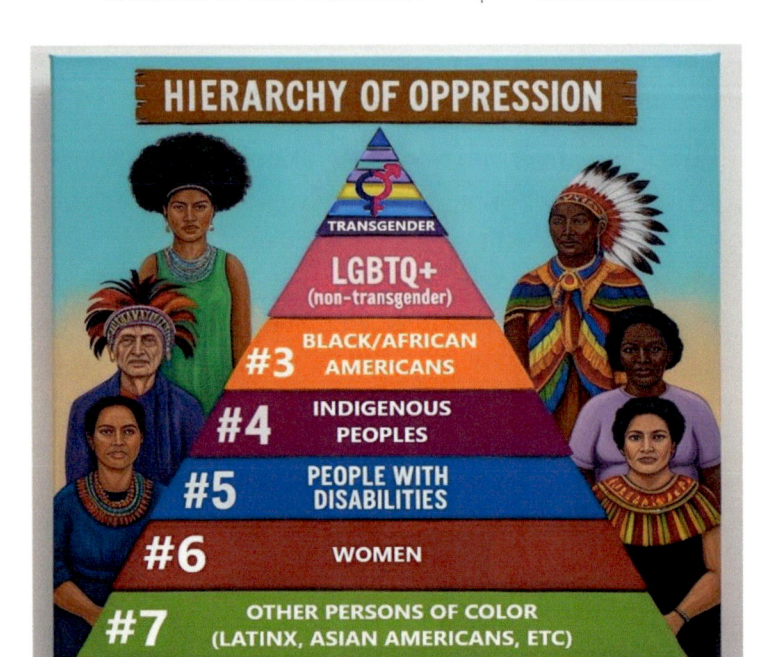

As illustrated above, per the underlying tenants of *intersectionality*, transgender individuals (especially transgender women of color) are considered among the most oppressed due to the combination of systemic discrimination, societal stigma, and violence they face.

A disciple of the *Church of Wokeism* would consider this informal hierarchy as highlighting the profound intersectional challenges faced by these oppressed groups. Ultimately, the concept of ranking oppression is inherently controversial, as it risks oversimplifying complex social dynamics and can inadvertently create divisiveness rather than unity among marginalized groups.

For example, Kimberlé Crenshaw (whose work predates Wokeism) would vehemently oppose a hierarchy of oppression. In her paper she states:

> *"Because the intersectional experience is greater than the sum of racism and sexism, any analysis that does not take intersectionality into account cannot sufficiently address the particular manner in which Black women are subordinated."*
> (Kimberlé Crenshaw, 1989)

Philosopher and civil rights leader, Audre Lorde, published the work *The Master's Tools Will Never Dismantle the Master's House* (1979). In it she also challenges the idea of ranking oppressions or oppressed groups, focusing instead on solidarity across differences:

> *"There is no hierarchy of oppression… As a Black, lesbian, feminist, socialist, poet, mother, warrior, I am not free while any woman is unfree, even when her shackles are very different from my own."*
> (Audre Lorde, 1979)

The Hierarchy in Action

Despite these stated objections to a "Hierarchy of Oppression" (which is also formally rejected within The Church of Wokeism), the reality is that such a hierarchy is created, nonetheless. This is perhaps another great irony of Wokeism: it rejects hierarchical structures, while at the same time its very existence and the crudeness of its framework incentivizes them to form.

The limitations and crude implementation of certain DEI programs affirm this stark reality. In many corporate and governmental diversity initiatives, organizations often prioritize gender and sexual orientation, particularly for underrepresented groups such as lesbian women. The idea behind this is to support historically marginalized groups that have faced systemic disadvantages.

For example, in large tech companies, many diversity policies currently focus on recruiting women and LGBTQ individuals. Critics of these policies claim that such programs often place gender or sexual orientation diversity ahead of racial considerations. A gay woman, therefore, is far more likely to be selected for a diversity-focused role than a Black man, especially in industries where LGBTQ+ representation is a significant priority.

Funding imbalances also exist along the "oppression hierarchy." Significant financing disparity for healthcare initiatives have emerged in the context of LGBTQ+ health (which is higher on the "oppression hierarchy") versus racially specific health disparities.

For instance, certain LGBTQ+ healthcare programs in 2019 (particularly those concerned with HIV prevention and gender-affirming care) received significant federal funding through the *Ryan White HIV/AIDS Program*. However, funding for programs specifically targeting health outcomes for Black men, such as those addressing prostate cancer or mental health challenges tied to racial trauma, has historically been less robust. Advocacy groups, including *The National Black Men's Health Network*, have pointed out this imbalance, where LGBTQ+ health programs often receive more media attention and funding than those addressing Black male health. (*The Atlantic*, 2020).

Far less consequential, but in television and film there has been "diversity lopsidedness" as well. Over the last decade there has been a noticeable push for LGBTQ+ representation, with networks and streaming services focusing on *lesbian, trans, and bisexual women*. For instance, "Orange Is the New

Black" (2013–2019) became a cultural phenomenon, with lesbian women of color (like Laverne Cox, a trans woman) receiving significant visibility. This series was praised for "elevating queer women's stories." However, critiques from Black male critics have highlighted that, while lesbian representation flourished, Black male representation, especially in media centered around racial struggles (like police brutality) often remained marginalized or misrepresented. For instance, "The Hate U Give" (2018), a film about Black youth and police violence, was met with praise but faced fewer mainstream awards and attention than LGBTQ+ stories. (*The Atlantic, 2019 | The Guardian, 2020*).

Finally, within the broader LGBTQ+ rights movement, Black women have frequently criticized that the organization has focused heavily on gay women's issues (especially in terms of visibility), overshadowing racial justice issues that Black men face.

One example is Mara Keisling, a prominent transgender rights activist, calling attention to the discrepancies between racial and gender justice. Her work helped push for transgender rights, but Black men (especially those affected by mass incarceration) have often been sidelined in the conversations within LGBTQA+ spaces that prioritize gender identity over racial struggles. This discrepancy has been pointed out particularly by activists in the *Black Lives Matter* movement, who argue that issues affecting Black men (such as police brutality) often receive far less focus by advocacy groups as well as mainstream media and corporate alike. *(The Guardian, 2019).*

Woke Diagnosis

To steelman the Woke argument, there is a need to bring awareness and support for individuals and groups in our society that are marginalized or oppressed. Intersectionality instructs us that, due to multiple disparate oppressions at play, individuals may face layers of repression.

However, critics allege that "Woke" attempts to address intersectionality unintentionally install "oppression hierarchies" that favor one group of oppressed persons over others. This further divides our society and accomplishes more harm than good.

We must find a constructive way for *metamodern synthesis* whereby society faces the challenges of oppression without marginalizing others in the process.

"No one is more hated than he who speaks the truth."
— **Plato**

IDENTITY POLITICS, WHITE PRIVILEGE, & RACISM

Without further ado, let's dive into the meat of this discourse and discuss the claims, aims, and solutions proposed by the new Woke religion.

We shall start with racism. Wokeism initially started as a "wake up call" to bring attention to racial prejudice and discrimination impacting African Americans. But the term has dramatically shifted; it now goes far beyond awareness to political activism and Progressive ideology for a myriad of issues. However, let's zero in on Wokeism's most current perspective of racism.

The Paragon of Wokeness

Arguably, the greatest advocate for Woke theology is Robin DiAngelo—sociologist, diversity consultant, and author of *White Fragility: Why It's So Hard for White People to Talk About Racism*. In her best-selling book, she argues that racism is a system of power and privilege that operates at both individual and structural levels. DiAngelo suggests that all white people, regardless of their personal intentions, are socialized into a system that privileges *whiteness* and disadvantages people of color. This socialization, she argues, leads to behaviors that perpetuate racial inequality.

Her focus is on how white people contribute to maintaining this system of racial inequality through their actions, attitudes, and reactions, particularly in situations where race and racism are discussed. In this sense, DiAngelo highlights the need for white people to reflect on their role within systemic racism and to challenge the behaviors and attitudes that support it. DiAngelo states:

> *"The status quo in the United States is racism; and it is comfortable for me, as a white person, to live in a racist society."* (DiAngelo, 2020)

To sustain the momentum of BLM from the 2018 protests, DiAngelo insists it must become "uncomfortable" for white people to continue to benefit from racist systems:

> *"We've got to start making it uncomfortable and figuring out what supports we're going to put in place to help us continue to be uncomfortable. Because the forces of comfort are quite seductive."* (DiAngelo, 2020)

The language used by DiAngelo is interesting. The book goes on to explain that while Whites can never "get over" their racism; they can learn to accept it and grow from it. A notable aspect of the vernacular is how akin to religious phraseology the semantic tones resonate. "White racism" is the new "original sin" (Catholicism). It cannot be escaped but only accepted. And whereas the Pentecostal Christian "language" would prescribe Jesus to cover over one's sin(s), DiAngelo posits no such claim for the Woke religion. There is no "overcoming" the sin of racism; there is no divine power to wash it clean. It simply must be accepted. Perhaps, though it is not explicitly stated by DiAngelo, through penance one might be sanctified in due course. The Woke religion is fairly new, so time will tell how its creed evolves.

What's also worth noting is that DiAngelo, the variable paragon of Wokeism (at least with respect to the field of white racism), is, herself, *white*. One may find amusement that the loudest and most vocal exemplar of the racism-decrying sub-doctrine of Wokeism is not in fact a person of color. A white woman has co-opted the space which might otherwise be chaired by a Black person. From a Progressive lens, this seems ironic.

There is a far more pernicious issue at hand with the overall philosophy. It is divisive. It draws bifurcation lines down the middle and separates white from black (literally). It exclusively focuses on RACE as a demarcation point between peoples, placing undue emphasis on identity politics instead of a person's individual merits, character, or moral fiber.

Is MLK's Dream Dead in the Woke Church?

I don't know about you, but I have deep and heartfelt memories of learning about the original *raison d'être* for the US Civil Rights Movement:

> *"I have a dream that my four little children will one day live in a nation where they will not be judged by the color of their skin but by the content of their character. [...] I have a dream that one day every valley shall be exalted, every hill and mountain shall be made low, the rough places will be made plain, and the crooked places will be made straight, and the glory of the Lord shall be revealed, and all flesh shall see it together."* (Martin Luther King, Jr, 1963)

Not too long ago, it was the North Star for our country to be "color blind" with respect to someone's race, creed, gender, or identity. To evaluate one's value based on WHO THEY WERE – their moral essence – was divine!

Wokeism has strayed far afield from this beautiful vision. Wokeism has caused society at large to slip backwards, rather than taking great strides forward. Instead of being a country dedicated to merit and virtue, we have become overly obsessed with race and gender. The *Church of Wokeism* desperately seeks to point out all the differences between peoples instead of what unites and strengthens them! The Church's rhetoric uses words of bifurcation and distinction. All its worship is made to that which separates white from black and the "faithful" from the "unrighteous."

With the heavy hand of religion comes the purists, legalists, and extremists. For all religions have their "poles" – with the disinterested fair-weather "Sunday Churchgoers" on one end and the overly-ardent "Church Ladies" and zealous deacons in the other. Sadly, it is the latter group that makes all the rules, ushers out the commands, and doles out punishment for the unfaithful. Even other Woke disciples are often admonished, or even demonized, for failing to step into line quickly enough. The common expression for this phenomenon is "the Left eats their own."

For example, a liberal student at the University of Virginia School of Medicine named Kieran Bhattacharya was thrown off campus after he questioned a black speaker's definition of *microaggressions* during a collegiate panel discussion. Within a few weeks, as a result of the fallout from Bhattacharya's question about microaggressions, the administration branded him a threat to the university and banned him from campus. He is now suing UVA for violating his First Amendment rights. Here are the details of his story:

> "Thank you for your presentation," said Bhattacharya, according to an audio recording of the event. "I had a few questions, just to clarify your definition of *microaggressions*. Is it a requirement, to be a victim of microaggression, that you are a member of a marginalized group?"
>
> Adams replied that it wasn't a requirement.
>
> Bhattacharya suggested that this was contradictory, since a slide in her presentation had defined microaggressions as negative interactions with members of marginalized groups. Adams and Bhattacharya then clashed for a few minutes about how to define the term. It was a polite disagreement. Adams generally maintained that microaggression theory was a broad and important topic and that the slights caused real harm. Bhattacharya expressed a scientific skepticism that a microaggression could be distinguished from an unintentionally rude statement. His doubts were well-founded given that microaggression theory is not a particularly rigorous concept.
>
> But Nora Kern, an assistant professor who helped to organize the event, thought Bhattacharya's questions were a bit too pointed. Immediately following the panel, she filed a "professionalism concern card"—a kind of record of a student's violations of university policy.

"This student asked a series of questions that were quite antagonistic toward the panel," wrote Kern. "He pressed on and stated one faculty member was being contradictory. His level of frustration/anger seemed to escalate until another faculty member defused the situation by calling on another student for questions. I am shocked that a med student would show so little respect toward faculty members. It worries me how he will do on wards."

According to Bhattacharya's lawsuit, the concern card generated interest from an assistant dean in the medical school, who emailed him and offered to meet. The assistant dean assured him that "I simply want to help you understand and be able to cope with unintended consequences of conversations."

Bhattacharya responded that contrary to anyone's assertions, he had not lost his temper or become frustrated with the panel:

"Your observed discomfort of me from wherever you sat was not at all how I felt. I was quite happy that the panel gave me so much time to engage with them about the semantics regarding the comparison of microaggressions and barbs. I have no problems with anyone on the panel; I simply wanted to give them some basic challenges regarding the topic. And I understand that there is a wide range of acceptable interpretations on this. I would be happy to meet with you at your convenience to discuss this further."

Then a dean of student affairs asked to meet as well. Meanwhile, the Academic Standards and Achievement Committee met to discuss the concern card. This committee voted to send Bhattacharya a written reminder to "show mutual respect" to faculty members and "express yourself appropriately." The committee also suggested that he get counseling.

On November 26, this suggestion became a mandate: The student was informed that he *must* be evaluated by psychological services before returning to classes. Bhattacharya repeatedly asked university officials to clarify what exactly he was accused of, under whose authority his counseling had been mandated, and why his enrollment status was suddenly in doubt, according to the lawsuit. These queries only appear to have made UVA officials more determined to punish him. Bhattacharya's mounting frustration with these baseless accusations of unspecified wrongdoings was essentially treated as evidence that he was guilty. At his hearing, he was accused of being "extremely defensive" and ordered to change his "aggressive, threatening behavior"

He was ultimately suspended for "aggressive and inappropriate interactions in multiple situations." On December 30, UVA police ordered him to leave campus. (Reason, 2021)

Another case of the Left "eating its own" concerns the Leftist group, *Gays Against Groomers*. The mission statement of this organization cites its opposition to the sexualization, indoctrination, and medicalization of children under the guise of LGBTQ+ advocacy. The group asserts that these practices are harmful to children and do not represent the values or interests of the broader LGBTQ+ community. However, because the views of this Progressive group are not quite as "Woke" as the *Church of Wokeism* requires to be considered pure, they have been cast out.

Specifically, *Gays Against Groomers* has been vilified by the Woke Left through accusations of promoting anti-LGBTQ+

rhetoric and aligning with far-right groups, with many zealots labeling them as a "hate group" despite their LGBTQ+ identity. Social media platforms like PayPal and Venmo have banned the group, citing violations of community guidelines; deacons within the Church accuse them of enabling discriminatory policies targeting transgender rights.

However, returning to the relevant topic of assertions of racism, *Slate.com* put out a noteworthy article in August of 2018 titled *Why White Liberals Are So Unwilling to Recognize Their Own Racism.* In it, the author seems almost confused for a moment on his own woke ideology. Recognizing, in a rare moment of lucidity while discussing microaggressions as a form of racism, he reflectively asks:

> "I think we might want a different word [for racism], rather than just adding 'avowed'. It seems like if we're re-conceptualizing what racism is, or at least how it's commonly defined, maybe [we] want a different word for racist politicians versus KKK members. Or maybe [we] don't because it's all part of a gradation. Or maybe it's not. I'm just thinking out loud..." (Isaac Chotiner, Slate.com, 2018)

Sadly, none of the other woke evangelists ever got this introspective memo from Chotiner. Rather, the blanket term "racist" has snowballed into becoming the singular epithet hurled at unbelievers so much that it seems to lose its meaning.

I recently read my eight-year daughter the story of *The Boy Who Cried Wolf*:

> A young shepherd who feels bored and wants attention falsely cries out that a wolf is attacking his sheep. When villagers rush to his aid, they find no

wolf and realize he has lied. He pulls this prank two more times, laughing harder each time. However, soon after, a real wolf appears and threatens his flock. This time, when he calls for help ("WOLF! WOLF! WOLF!"), the villagers don't believe him, thinking it's another false alarm. As a result, the wolf kills the boy and eats the sheep.

The lesson is painfully obvious. When the Woke Mob cries "*racist*!" over and over and over again – about this microaggression or that one, about an insufficient number of dark(er) skin band-aids, or about the pay gap between races – society will turn a deaf ear to REAL racism when it appears.

The last point to bring up about the Woke Religion's obsession with identity politics and its threadbare adjudications of "racism" is that it has the OPPOSITE impact on helping the plight of the Black community. Irony, again, is not a stranger to the regiment and direct outcomes of Woke hysteria.

In his book *Woke Racism: How a New Religion Has Betrayed Black America*, Professor John McWhorter argues that **neoracism**, disguised as *antiracism*, is hurting Black communities all across the US. According to McWhorter, the problem is that a well-meaning but pernicious form of antiracism has become "not a progressive ideology, but rather a religion."

McWhorter shows how this new religion's claims to "dismantle racist structures" infantilize Black Americans, set Black students up for failure, and pass policies that disproportionately damage Black communities. He shares scripts and encouragement with those trying to deprogram friends and family, and offers a roadmap to justice:

"Many people are under the impression that change for Black America can only happen in a real way if the rest of America is united in a profound understanding of what Black people have been through. This means that they see battling power differentials wielded by whites as central to intellectual and artistic endeavor, and any questioning of this as "white supremacy." I question these lines of reasoning—I want true change for Black America, but do not see this kind of psychosocial reprogramming as necessary to it.

Much of *the new antiracist paradigm hurts Black people in the name of helping us*. It thus should be resisted, as should, overall, the simplistic idea that battling power differentials must be our dominant endeavor as opposed to one of many. Thus: when a vocal minority of people in your organization insist that its whole *modus operandi* be transformed in order to hold battling power differentials as the MAIN goal, we must all develop the bravery to tell them no—and be fully prepared for them to call you a white supremacist in response.

Time passes, and what's important is that people like this not be under the impression that they can get anything they desire by calling the rest of us something awful. Most people do not agree with this form of wokeness; it won't do to pretend we do just to avoid being yelled at." (McWhorter, 2022).

So, what lessons (if any) can be learned from all this? The *Church of Wokeism* preaches division; its teachers stand on grand pulpits and decry that the Great Devil of Racism is all around us. It is *in* us! It is whiteness manifest. What is the effect of this fire-and-brimstone testimony? Many argue that due to the incendiary language of Church acolytes, race relations have not improved one mite since 2015. In fact, they have gone significantly backwards. Why? This regression has not happened *despite* the spiritual efforts of The Church of Wokeism, but BECAUSE of its divisive preachings!

Let's consider a short history to gauge the results. The election of Barack Obama as the first Black President in 2008 was seen as a symbol of great progress for the Black community—and one would think that this would positively indicate that America is not quite as ignorant and racist as a Church of Wokeism deacon would exclaim.

However, fast-forward eight short years. After the proliferation of Wokeism, race relations became more visibly polarized, driven in part by the rise of movements such as BLM, which gained momentum following racialized incidents such as the shooting of Michael Brown in Ferguson, Missouri, and the deaths of other Black individuals at the hands of police. Between 2016 – 2024, the social media era amplified tensions around racial injustice through a radical Woke lens.

But post-2015, especially with the election of Donald Trump in 2016, race relations became marked by heightened political polarization, with tensions around immigration, nationalism, and racial identity playing out regularly in public discourse. The purported rise of "white nationalist" movements and backlash to movements for racial justice signaled a deeper divide in public attitudes toward race as reaction/counterreaction forces raced to the poles of their ideologies.

Comparatively, while racial tensions before 2015 were often framed around issues of overt discrimination and inequality, after 2015, they became intertwined with debates about identity politics, systemic racism, and the role of law enforcement. Social movements became more vocal, focusing on addressing structural racism rather than just individual acts of prejudice, while conversations about reparations and racial reconciliation gained prominence.

Despite all the talk of action by the Progressive Left, economic inequality, racial profiling, and voter suppression continued to affect minority communities, especially Black Americans. Thus, while there were moments of progress, race relations post-2015 reflected an ongoing struggle and a deep divide. Under the banner of Wokeism, the plight of the African American in the United States *regressed*.

The "Woke" movement has, in most every way, made race relations worse by exclusively focusing on identity politics, which divide us all. It has embraced polarization, and in doing so has created an ingrained culture of deep division.

Moreover, like a 'nosy church lady' hiding in the bushes shouting "SIN! SIN!" upon witnessing Jimmy stick his tongue down his girlfriend Jenny's throat, the Woke obsession with calling out perceived injustices (including "microaggressions") fosters an environment of *cancel culture*. Within this paradigm of hypersensitivity, people are publicly shamed or ostracized for comments or actions that are seen as racially insensitive, *even if they were not intended as harmful.*

The tragic emphasis on identity politics, where individuals are categorized based solely on their race instead of their unique individual characteristics, creates new forms of division rather than unity. Doing so alienates those who might otherwise be open to conversations about racial equity.

Finally, Wokeness tends to create *bogeymen* and employs symbolic actions (like renaming buildings or statues – or especially tearing down statutes) rather than pushing for substantive policy changes which would move the needle and fight actual racism.

"Freedom begins where ignorance ends."
— ***Victor Hugo***

OPPRESSION OF WOMEN

The original women's rights movement of the 19th and early 20th centuries primarily focused on achieving equality and combating systemic sexism of men against women. However, since then, women as a class identity have been permitted into the great and welcoming halls of the *Church of Wokeism*. The movement has evolved into a broader "new woke feminism" that emphasizes inclusivity and *intersectionality*, sometimes prioritizing the affirmation of trans women's identities in ways critics argue might sideline or undermine issues uniquely affecting biological women.

Woke ideology, particularly as it relates to the oppression of women and the core tenets of feminism, now centers on addressing *intersecting systems of discrimination*, often emphasizing inclusivity and the acknowledgment of diverse experiences. Feminist principles within this framework seek to dismantle patriarchal structures while incorporating a broader understanding of how their *class identity* (race, sexuality, etc.) also intersects with more traditional gender-based oppression.

The Women's Right Movement

The women's rights movement in America began in earnest with the *Seneca Falls Convention of 1848*, where activists like Elizabeth Cady Stanton and Lucretia Mott demanded equal rights, particularly suffrage. This struggle culminated in the *19th Amendment in 1920*, granting women the right to vote.

During the mid-20th century, the *second-wave feminist movement*, led by figures like Betty Friedan and Gloria Steinem, expanded the fight to issues such as workplace equality, reproductive rights, and combating gender stereotypes.

Third-wave feminism emerged in the early 1990s and focused on challenging traditional ideas of womanhood, emphasizing individuality, *intersectionality*, and *diversity*. It sought to start to incorporate issues like race and sexuality while critiquing second-wave feminism for being overly centered on the experiences of white, middle-class women.

Today, *Woke feminism*, which gained prominence in the 2010s, builds on third-wave principles but greatly intensifies the focus on *intersectionality and inclusivity*. It places almost exclusive emphasis on LGBTQ+ rights, particularly transgender inclusion, and critiques systemic oppression more broadly. Critics often argue it shifts away from addressing sex-based issues traditionally at the core of feminism.

Fourth-wave feminism (aka "Woke feminism"), underscores how systemic inequalities affect women differently based on other facets of their identity. For instance, it argues that white women and women of color experience sexism differently due to the compounding effects of racism. This approach builds on Kimberlé Crenshaw's theory of *intersectionality*, which highlights how multiple axes of oppression interconnect to shape unique experiences.

In real world application, what this unfortunately does is cause the "hierarchy of oppression" to manifest in varying ways. For example, a person of color or transgender person may often receive preferential treatment over "just a woman" because the LGBTQA+ person or transgender person experiences "heightened levels of intersectionality-based prejudice." As such, a Black transgender woman has won the "Woke lottery" with respect to preferential treatment within this ideology—which, in fairness, is done benevolently to attempt to "make up" for this disenfranchised subgroup being unfairly biased against by the rest of "Non-Woke" society. However, as a result, a white woman may find herself passed up for a promotion or not hired at all—with preference given to the bisexual man or trans woman (biologically male).

This, in turn, often creates a self-defeating outcome of fourth-wave feminism—as under this framework men (particularly Black men) are often prioritized over white or straight women. Thus, depending on the circumstance, the aims of feminism (to promote and champion women's rights) are ironically often thwarted by the very movement that proports to promote women.

Additionally, The *Church of Wokeism* now often castigates "traditional feminism" (as well as other precedent waves of feminism) for being historically dominated by white, middle-class women, calling for a more expansive and inclusive approach and a greater focus on race and sexuality. Many staunch feminists of the 1990s and early 2000s face vitriol and "banishment" from Woke circles for no longer being in "the in-group." Once again, as the saying goes: *the left eats their own*.

This phenomenon reminds me of whenever members of my former Evangelical church would choose to "color outside the lines" when expressing their faith in Jesus. If Jesus didn't fit the exact box that the Church put Him into, these individuals were "sternly spoken to" – or, quite often, asked to leave the Church. A rigid, faith-based philosophy often has no patience for "free thinkers" – even when those free thinkers simply stood fast and thought the way they always had before the Church decided to "evolve" and move forward in their 'reformed understanding of God.'

For that is often what happens – the tomes and preaching at the pulpit changes, yet the practitioner is often left flat-footed, working from an "old copy" of the hymns, liturgies, and formal creed. But to stay faithful, you better "keep up" or "ship out." After all, you're either with us or you're against us!

Tensions Within Feminism

A point of contention in *Woke* discussions about women's oppression arises with the inclusion of transgender women in feminist spaces. Critics argue that redefining womanhood to include individuals assigned male at birth dilutes the focus on sex-based oppression and rights, such as those related to reproductive health. Proponents within the Church, however, stress that transgender women also face misogyny and violence, arguing for solidarity across all individuals who experience gender-based discrimination.

Celebrated children's author, J.K. Rowling, is of the (now highly contentious) "second wave feminism" persuasion. She has spoken quite publicly—facing significant Woke pushback—about the virtues of feminism as a movement rooted in the recognition and protection of women's rights and identities. She has emphasized the importance of acknowledging biological realities in defining womanhood, arguing that **"woman is not a costume"** or an abstract idea. Rowling has also highlighted the challenges women face globally, from misogyny to online abuse, and called for solidarity in addressing these systemic issues. She believes feminism should remain focused on dismantling patriarchy while ensuring women's unique struggles are not erased:

> 'Woman' is not a costume. 'Woman' is not an idea in a man's head. 'Woman' is not a pink brain, a liking for Jimmy Choos, or any of the other sexist ideas now somehow touted as progressive.
>
> [...] I've read all the arguments about femaleness not residing in the sexed body, and the assertions that biological women don't have common experiences, and I find them, too, deeply misogynistic and regressive. (Rowling, 2020)

Expanding Feminist Goals

Modern feminism within the *Church of Wokeism's* "fourth wave feminism" currently extends far beyond legal equality to address cultural and structural inequalities. It emphasizes issues like workplace discrimination, gender-based violence, and access to healthcare while also advocating for the rights of marginalized groups based on their sexual identity, such as non-binary individuals and sex workers. This new *Woke Feminist* movement challenges traditional notions of femininity, pushing for societal acceptance of diverse gender expressions and identities.

Overall, the *Church of Wokeism* has utterly reshaped traditional, second-wave, and even third-wave feminism to prioritize inclusivity and intersectionality above all else. Scholars like bell hooks [sic] (*pen name of Gloria Jean Watkins*), Roxane Gay, and Judith Butler provide deeper insight into contemporary feminist thought within the Woke age of new feminism.

Critics of fourth-wave feminism ("Woke feminism") argue that its focus on sexual identity and inclusivity, while important in their own right, serves to significantly divert attention from systemic issues that disproportionately affect women globally, such as economic inequality, reproductive rights, and gender-based violence. Some claim it risks diluting the feminist agenda by prioritizing individual identity over collective action against patriarchy. Others highlight tensions over redefining womanhood to include transgender identities, suggesting this certainly undermines efforts to address sex-based oppression, thereby alienating those who seek to maintain feminism's profound and enlightened focus on biological women's experiences.

In short, **the Woke movement has co-opted feminism from the feminists!** It did this in the same insidious way as it co-opted the term 'Woke' from the Black community—by slowly turning up the dial of relativism until holistic perspective by the original group making it up was completely eroded away. With that said, let's now turn a deconstructive eye to the substrate of transgenderism within the Woke movement and round out the edges a bit more…

TRANSGENDERISM

As described, the Progressive Left co-opted a Black word that was originally purposed to "wake people up" to injustices in the African American community. It now is a shotgun term to give activist credence to any marginalized group.

The most politically charged woke flavor of the day is "transgender rights." The *Church of Wokeism* has summarily decreed (although unofficially) that the transgender community is the most marginalized group in the unofficial and completely-off-the-record hierarchy of unequal power dynamics. And the closer to the top of the oppression pyramid a group is, the more preferential treatment it receives in the Church's gospel. Put another way, the reason this topic is critical is because if Wokeism is the archetypal "poster child" of Postmodernism, then Transgenderism is Wokeism's "poster child."

Here is the central argument with respect to transgender activism: *gender is not binary*.

I realize the irony of questioning this assertion given that this book's central thesis is that no issue is ever truly binary— and it is important to consider a nuanced approach to complex topics. So let me strongman the "trans rights" position and couch it in the language of the Holy Church:

Transgenderism Defined

The assertion that gender is non-binary is a central tenet of "woke" ideology. Wokeism places a high value on identity markers such as gender identity. The term "gender binary" refers to the long-standing biological axiom that there are only two genders: male and female. "Non-binary" is a term used to describe people who don't identify exclusively as male or female. Non-binary people may identify as both, neither, or a combination of the two. For example, someone who identifies as non-binary might feel more masculine on some days and more feminine on others.

Furthermore, transgenderism emphasizes that a person's gender identity is a deeply personal experience that may not align with the sex assigned at birth, and that respecting someone's self-identified gender, including using their preferred pronouns, is crucial to creating an inclusive and supportive environment. This framework would also highlight the importance of access to gender-affirming healthcare, gender-affirming surgeries, gender-affirming medication (i.e. puberty blockers), and advocating against discrimination faced by transgender individuals.

The natural outcome of these arguments is that males and females may be "born in the wrong body" and often desire/require assistance from the medical community to "fix" what nature screwed up. Thus, the euphemism "gender affirming care" has recently been advocated for both adults as well as children to aid in these medical treatments, such as surgical procedures, cosmetic alterations, and chemical applications to aid in biological reversals/augmentations.

Transgenderism Harms LGB & Feminism

There are a number of concerns with this ideology worth discussing, not least of which is the ethical ramifications of providing such "care" (described above) to young(er) children.

But a central issue critics spotlight is the damage Wokeism specifically causes to the lesbian, gay, and bisexual ("LGB") community. For example, by encouraging a young male who demonstrates effeminate characteristics to then transform into "a trans girl" instead of simply admitting they likely are gay does a great disservice to the homosexual movement. Many suggest the cultural zeitgeist of pushing transgenderism on children takes gay rights activism back decades.

The cultural fervor for transgenderism greatly diminishes the long-fought normalcy of homosexuality in society. Instead, the suggestion is that it's a stigma to be gay, or that it's much better to simply consider oneself the other gender and use medicine/surgery to "fix" the gender allotted at birth. With transgenderism so normalized (and often encouraged), homosexuality takes a proverbial backseat.

Critics insist the transgender movement, and its associated societal pressures, often influence young men and women during a period of puberty or sexual confusion. Heavily influencing and encouraged rhetoric insinuates, for example: *"if you're a boy attracted to another boy, you're not gay; instead, wouldn't it be easier if you simply became a girl so that your desires were more normalized in the body of another gender?"* Thus, wokeism subliminally implies, through gentle pressure, that it's better for some to be a trans girl than a gay man. Many critics find this overall sentiment wildly disrespectful to the homosexual community, which has worked so hard for decades to achieve cultural acceptance and normalcy.

In recent years, the relationship between the homosexual and transgender movements within the **LGBTQIA+** (**L**esbian, **G**ay, **B**isexual, **T**ransgender, **Q**ueer or **Q**uestioning, **I**ntersex, **A**sexual, **+** Other Identities) spectrum has also sparked significant debate, with many groups expressing concern that transgender issues dominate the agenda at the expense of lesbian, gay, and bisexual (LGB) representation. One such organization, the *LGB Alliance*, was founded in 2019 in the UK to advocate specifically for the interests of lesbians, gay men, and bisexuals. The group contends that the inclusion of transgender issues within the broader LGBTQIA+ movement shifts focus away from sexual orientation and towards gender identity, creating tensions in policy and advocacy.

Prominent feminist and lesbian activists, such as Sheila Jeffreys and Julie Bindel, have voiced similar concerns, particularly around the implications of transgender activism for women-only spaces and the definition of lesbian identity. These critics argue that expanding the definition of "woman" to include individuals who identify as female but were assigned male at birth can undermine the ability of lesbians to organize around shared experiences of biological sex-based oppression. This perspective has been especially contentious in debates over the inclusion of transgender women in women's sports and shelters, as well as in the discourse surrounding gender-affirming healthcare.

With respect to feminism, famed author of the *Harry Potter* series of books, J.K. Rowling, has voiced significant concerns over policies allowing self-identification of gender without medical or legal safeguards, asserting that they could potentially harm women's rights. She described the current period as one of heightened misogyny, exacerbated by pressures for women to concede that "there is no material difference between trans women and themselves," which she and other feminists find regressive and alienating.

Within academic and activist circles, many gay and lesbian advocates have noted that the LGBTQIA+ movement's strong focus on transgender issues risks overshadowing the distinct challenges faced by homosexual individuals. Concerns are often raised about policy priorities, such as the balance between addressing gender identity versus sexual orientation in healthcare, education, and anti-discrimination laws. For example, debates about the rights of gender-nonconforming children have sometimes polarized communities, with differing views on whether certain interventions align with the broader goals of the LGBTQIA+ movement.

These debates highlight the complexities and evolving dynamics of LGBTQIA+ advocacy, as the movement seeks to balance solidarity with acknowledging the unique needs of its diverse members. While some individuals and groups advocate for a more unified front, others believe that focusing on distinct identities is essential to ensuring that the challenges of all subgroups within the community are addressed.

Interview of Timothy Baxter

As I am cisgender, male, and white, I recognize I am likely not equipped to have such a nuanced conversation with adequate perspective. I do not want to be accused of failing to bring alternative perspectives to the table. And I certainly don't want to pretend to have the knowledge or life experience required to represent the gay community.

As such, I interviewed a friend and colleague, Timothy Baxter, to weigh in on this topic. Mr. Baxter is a successful entrepreneur, a former candidate for New Hampshire State Senate, and a proud member of the homosexual community. What follows is my interview with him.

> **ME**: Tim, thanks so much for joining me today. Do you mind please sharing your viewpoints on identity politics in today's climate.
>
> **TIM**: Well, I think identity politics are a sort of political weapon – just like calling folks homophobic, xenophobic, or racist. The Left uses identity politics as a weapon to just bludgeon their political opponents, or whoever's in their way. And you see this sort of visceral anger when there's someone disagreeing with them that's in one of these groups of people that the Left is saying are in a victim class (for example, if you are gay, or if you are Black or Hispanic).
>
> It's kind of like *cultural religion* and it's lacking any substance on any of the key issues on education or the economy, inflation, etc. It's all a political game in their view. So, they want to just take all these components […] and shove them together.
>
> That's why I don't even call it LGBTQIA+. I call it "LGBTQIA plus infinity." Because that's kind of what it is. Because they don't actually see the nuances or really care about, you know, what someone's personal experiences are as a gay person or a transgender person. It's all about *the group*!

Like, I'm gay, right? But ... I also run a business! I want to start a family. I want to have kids. The fact that I'm gay is one of the *least* interesting things about me. But to the Democrat party, that's the only thing that matters. And if you don't regurgitate their language and use their identity [classification] – to be some nameless number in their class-based "Victim Oppression Olympics" or whatever it is – then they despise you.

ME: That's interesting. As a gay man, does 'Staying Woke' play a role in your life?

TIM: I think the problem is that the Democrat Party has become the party of wokeism. It's their base, right? They've lost a lot of these minority groups that they pretend to care about, and their base is sort of this highly educated upper middle class – single white ladies! Their base is no longer working in nine-to-five jobs; and 'the Woke' have stopped focusing on real issues that most people actually care about that are impacting them in their life. Instead, it's focused on a lot of these cultural identity politics issues. But that's not what motivates people!

ME: You said you feel your sexuality is the least interesting characteristic about you. It doesn't define you. Why, then, do you feel that identity groupings are what the Left focuses on the most? What is the point of trying to put you into the "gay" box? And do you think if you were Transgender you'd feel differently?

TIM: Well, one thing I'll bring up before I answer that question. I think one of the big differences maybe between being gay or bisexual and, say, transgender is that as a gay person, you don't know [that I'm gay]. Just consider my everyday routine. Most of what I do … I'm interacting with people as a business owner;

I'm talking to different people—whether it's investors or tenants or vendors, right? Or maybe it's on the weekend … I'm hanging out with people. There's the vast majority of people I might hang out with that have no idea that I'm gay, right? It doesn't come up—because I'm running my business. I'm creating value. I'm having fulfilling personal relationships.

But if you're transgender and you have to identify as a boy even though you're a girl – and you want everyone to perceive you as a man instead of a woman – that's probably much more likely to interfere with your daily life and your workplace and your business. And so, I think it is a totally different ball of wax!

And I think that's why too, there's a lot of Republican gay guys. A lot of that group, like myself, [find it] kind of hard to identify with transgender people in any way, shape, or form because it's so foreign. It's as foreign to me as you thinking about being gay. Like it's almost not comprehendible. And so, to lump all these things together [into the *LQBTQIA+* moniker], it's just … it is more of a *political lumping* than it is one that makes any real sense.

ME: Do you feel as a gay man that your rights, so to speak, have been marginalized by the trans community in any way?

TIM: I worry about that a lot more for the kids or people that are less confident than I am. I've always had a lot of confidence. So [when I was younger] it's not like my teacher may have convinced me that I was depressed because I'm not actually gay, I'm transgender or something like that.

However, I do worry that with all the wokeism injected into the schools that, on the margins, many children are the ones most struggling with their mental health.

Those are the kids that are maybe going to end up like guinea pigs for this woke ideology, whether that's with transgenderism or whether that's with critical race theory, whatever it is. So, I worry about that a lot more for the next generation that's coming up now.

But you brought up a question earlier and I didn't answer it. What was it again?

ME: In your own life, why do you think that Progressives choose to focus on your sexuality or, say, your identity group far more than they do your individual characteristics?

TIM: Well, I think that's probably because the Left doesn't like thinking of people as individuals. They like thinking of people as *groups*. They're uncomfortable with the notion that praising and rewarding someone when they succeed — or criticizing or helping a person grow if they fail. They want to make it all about the *collective*. And I think it's easier if we're not responsible to a large degree for our success or our failure. Then we can blame somebody else. So, they'll use it.

Maybe blame capitalists, or lately, you know, blame "the hierarchy" based solely on their physical traits— which would be the straight, white, cis male.

Blame them if you're struggling, right? It's not because of terrible economic policies, but it's because straight white men are destroying the economy or something. *They're* the ones destroying your lives or taking away your rights! *They're* marginalizing you. Maybe *they're* not paying you the same percentage because you're a woman. Or because you're Black, right? It's not your fault. It's all because of the straight white men! *They're* destroying the economy. *They're* keeping you down.

So, I think marginalizing people by shoveling them into these collective groups can take away their agency. And then they can create a boogeyman of a certain type of class, which would be the straight white man typically.

ME: That brings up another question. Do you believe that these "boogeyman" that the Left create are specific attempts to try to thwart the American people from focusing their attention in a particular direction? Or do you think that it's generic misdirection and they just want to create havoc for havoc's sake?

TIM: So, I would say it's different depending on who you're talking about.

I think the most far left-wing types, like the university professors, these people are hardcore socialists, and they have completely embraced identity politics. They BELIEVE it. That's why wokeism, transgenderism, et cetera are strong movements in all the Ivy League colleges.

Whereas I think if you look at many of the politicians – look at the Democrat Party: a Pelosi, a Schumer, or the sort of center-left-wing aristocratic donor – those people, I think, use identity politics strictly as a useful weapon. I think it's very sinister how they use identity politics, and it allows the elites to distract people from their failures, in particular their economic failures.

And, so, I think there is a lot of the base that really believes [in Woke ideology], but I think the people in charge do not. For the politicians wokeism is more of a useful weapon—and it's pretty sinister, as I said before.

ME: Tim, thank you. I've enjoyed our chat.

Closing Thoughts

To conclude this overview of a highly sensitive issue in today's culture, *diversity* is critical: diversity of viewpoint and diversity of mindset.

It is very easy to let ideological "bubbles" and "echo chambers" influence (or even direct) one's perspective. Analyzing nuanced and multilayered topics with alternative perspectives is critical to get a comprehensive understanding. To that end, the *Church of Wokeism* rarely considers all sides of complex issues. Inviting dialogue and serious contemplation of sensitive topics with a diverse group of individuals that disagree (including in-group factions of LGBTQA+ that express differing viewpoints) often helps one reach a greater appreciation for the intricate web of nuance involved in such controversial topics.

"Doubt is not a pleasant condition, but certainty is absurd."
— ***Voltaire***

WALL STREET "GOES WOKE"

> *"Villains who twirl their moustaches are easy to spot; those who clothe themselves in good deeds are well-camouflaged." – Admiral Satie (ST:TNG, The Drumhead)*

The 1% vs the 99%

The year is 2011. It is early fall in New York City. The *Occupy Wall Street* (OWS) movement is in full swing. Thousands of people gather in tent camps and shake their fists at the pristine windows of Big Bank executives, nearly half a mile above their heads. It is a case of the rich against the poor, the proletariat vs. the bourgeoisie. The poor are many in number; the rich are few.

This was a populist movement of "the 99%" against the putrid corruption of the Big Banks and Big Corporations, "the 1%." The Federal Reserve along with giant corporate banks and their executives had swindled billions of dollars from the poor and middle class and created an almost incalculable wealth divide. And that was even before the bank bailouts of 2008. After that, the rich just got even richer and richer...and richer!

These protests were a direct response to growing economic inequality. Thousands were in attendance. The complaints focused heavily on the role of big banks in exacerbating income inequality, specifically in the aftermath of the 2008 financial crisis. Demonstrators sought to highlight issues such as corporate greed, financial deregulation, and the perceived influence of large financial institutions over government policy.

It didn't look good for the banks. The media was casting an eagle eye on their financial dealings. The talk of "overpaid executives" and "golden parachutes" was escalating fast. The dam looked ready to burst. The bankers were scared; history showed that poor and starving people didn't take too kindly to "fat cats" in their ivory towers. Were heads about to roll?

Turning of the Tide

However, without warning, everything changed. Like a light switch flipped, the massive media attention was suddenly directed elsewhere. The demonstrations ended. The protests ceased. The "tenters" packed up and left. The sins of the evil banking sector were apparently forgiven. Their massive executive bonuses were ignored. Their greed, corruption, and thievery were quietly swept under the rug.

Whatever could explain this turn of events?

Well, these very same banks and large corporations suddenly began to shift their public messaging and embrace certain aspects of progressive social movements, including, you guessed it – "Wokeism."

What a wild coincidence! What a change of heart. These bankers, once "the scum of the earth" not long prior now were "the good guys!" They had joined the fight for the underserved now. They were redeemed! They were *Woke*! Hallelujah. With the flick of a pen and a few dollars shuffled around, corporate giants like JP Morgan Chase and Bank of America implemented Diversity, Equity, and Inclusion (DEI) programs and launched marketing campaigns to align with social justice movements, including LGBTQ+ rights, anti-racism campaigns, and racial justice.

Now was this a genuine commitment to radical social justice or a strategic move to deflect blame and improve their public image? It's impossible to know for sure.

Timeline of Events

What follows is a specific play-by-play timeline of key events surrounding *Occupy Wall Street* and the epic rise of "Wokeism" in corporate America:

- **2008:** The global financial crisis hits, with the collapse of major financial institutions, mass layoffs, and a deep recession. The U.S. government steps in with bailouts for banks and corporations, leaving many Americans angry over the perceived unfairness of the situation. This sets the stage for Occupy Wall Street and the criticism of the "1%" who were seen as benefiting while the broader population suffered.

- **September 17, 2011:** Occupy Wall Street begins in Zuccotti Park, New York City. The movement grows rapidly, with demonstrations spreading to cities across the U.S. Protesters decry the concentration of wealth and power in the hands of a few elite corporations and individuals, focusing specifically on the practices of big banks and financial institutions.

- **October 2011:** Bank of America, JPMorgan Chase, and other large banks face increasing scrutiny as they are seen as emblematic of corporate greed. The "We Are the 99%" slogan becomes iconic, with protesters demanding greater financial transparency, accountability, and systemic reform.

- **November 2011:** JPMorgan Chase is recognized as a leader in LGBTQ+ workplace equality, scoring 100% on the *Human Rights Campaign (HRC) Corporate Equality Index (CEI)*. They begin to offer inclusive benefits such as health insurance for same-sex domestic partners and supported LGBTQ+ employee resource groups.

- **December 2011:** Bank of America features inclusive messaging in campaigns about diversity and community support. They also publicly oppose discriminatory legislation and support marriage equality.

- **2012:** Bank of America expands its *LGBTQ+ Pride Employee Network*, which provides resources and advocacy for LGBTQ+ employees and allies.

- **2012:** JPMorgan Chase bank sponsors Pride events in major cities, including New York and San Francisco.

- **2012:** Goldman Sachs supports LGBTQ+ advocacy events, such as *Out on the Street*, a leadership initiative focused on advancing LGBTQ+ professionals in finance.

- **2013**: JPMorgan Chase launches the *Advancing Black Pathways* program, aimed at promoting economic inclusion and creating pathways for Black Americans to access financial services, education, and career opportunities.

- **2013**: Goldman Sachs begins the *Launch With GS* program to support women and diverse entrepreneurs by providing capital, mentorship, and networking opportunities.

- **2012-2014:** Large banks like JPMorgan Chase, Citigroup, and Wells Fargo make efforts to distance themselves from the negative perceptions tied to their role in the financial crisis. Some start to publicly support more progressive causes, such as gender equality and environmental sustainability, but the core of the protests—opposition to economic inequality and the power of big banks—remains unresolved.

- **2014**: Bank of America announces its $1.5 billion commitment to community development, with a focus on programs benefiting low-income and minority communities.

- **2014**: Wells Fargo creates its *Racial and Ethnic Diversity Initiative*, focusing on increasing minority representation at all levels of the company.

- **2014**: Citigroup joins the *Human Rights Campaign's Corporate Equality Index*, making a public commitment to LGBT equality.

- **2014**: Goldman Sachs makes public statements supporting LGBTQ+ rights and diversity, including a commitment to support companies with diverse boards.

- **2015**: Citigroup announces it will provide financial services and lending programs to underserved minority communities, including support for minority-owned businesses.

- **2015**: Wells Fargo makes a public commitment to LGBTQ+ rights and, along with BOA, becomes one of the first major financial institutions to publicly support marriage equality in the U.S.A.

- **2015-2017:** As the conversation around social justice, identity politics, and corporate responsibility becomes more widespread, the language of "wokeism" begins to emerge in mainstream corporate America. In the wake of Occupy Wall Street and the growing influence of social movements, many companies, including large banks, begin to embrace corporate social responsibility (CSR) initiatives and publicly advocate for diversity, equity, and inclusion (DEI) policies. Companies like Goldman Sachs, JPMorgan Chase, and Bank of America implement more robust DEI initiatives, often as part of their broader corporate image.

- **2018-2020:** As social justice movements such as *Black Lives Matter* and *MeToo* gain traction, many corporations, including big banks, make public commitments to fighting systemic racism, gender inequality, and other social issues. Critics argue that these actions are often more about virtue signaling or "woke capitalism" than effecting real change. In some cases, large banks faced criticism for their investments in industries like fossil fuels or private prisons, which undermined their claims of being socially responsible.

- **2020-Present:** The COVID-19 pandemic and the protests following George Floyd's killing further accelerate the "woke" movement in corporate America, with many institutions—including banks—posting statements of solidarity with racial justice movements.

Correlation Speculation

There appears to be significant correlation between the rise of the *Occupy Wall Street* ("OWS") movement and the subsequent embrace of Wokeism by the Big Banks. After OWS, many large corporations, especially financial institutions, faced mounting public pressure to appear more socially responsible. Given the heavy criticism from movements like OWS, embracing diversity and inclusion, environmental sustainability, and other Progressive causes seems to have been an effective way to improve their public image and deflect criticism away from their role in perpetuating economic inequality and the financial exploitation of the poor and middle class.

Immediately following the breakup of *Occupy Wall Street*, social justice issues suddenly became increasingly central in public discourse, particularly with movements like *Black Lives Matter* and the *#MeToo* movement. Corporations—particularly big banks and weapons companies—began recognizing that their most vocal customers, employees, and investors were increasingly aligning with these values, which led them to adopt an array of "woke" policies. Yet, the question remains whether these companies were genuinely committed to tackling the systemic inequalities exposed by OWS or if they were simply adopting *Wokeism* to deflect blame and skirt responsibility for their actions. Corporate influence over politics and money persisted. The rich continued to get richer and the poor got poorer. In this sense, the embrace of "woke" values by banks could be seen as more of a response to public pressure rather than a genuine effort to address the structural issues that the Occupy movement highlighted.

Ultimately, the correlation between the OWS movement and the rise of "woke" corporate practices is extremely suspect. Critics argue that many of the core issues raised by OWS—economic inequality, financial corruption, the marriage of Big Banks and Big Government, and the concentration of power—remain largely unaddressed.

Interview of Kevin Maley

However, a narrative can only have so much depth. To seek greater perspective on this issue, I sat down with liberal political podcaster Kevin Maley, who was an active protestor during the *Occupy Wall Street* movement.

> **ME**: Kevin, thank you for sitting down with me. Do you want to share a little bit about yourself? How do you identify yourself? A liberal podcaster? A political pundit? What labels do you use?
>
> **KEVIN**: Yeah. I don't even know how to define myself. I've always associated myself with "the Left." I became politically aware and involved during the lead-up to the invasion of Iraq. This was before it started, but I just remember trying to read as much as possible about the Middle East, about the history of the region.

A really important book that I read at that time – this is probably the fall of 2002 – is this one *[he reaches behind him and grabs a book from the middle of a massively packed, white bookcase]*: it's a book called "*The Prize*" by Daniel Jurgen, which is about the history of the oil industry.

Long story short, I became against the invasion of Iraq. This is before the invasion started, but in the fall of 2002, there was basically a big propaganda campaign that had been started by the George W. Bush administration. And there's a push for Congress to ratify the invasion through the *2002 Authorization for the Use of Military Force*. So, I was involved in protests against the authorization for the use of force.

And then I was involved in protest against the war itself after the invasion had begun. Around that time I started reading a lot more dissident intellectuals. So, [I was reading] everything that I could get my hands on by Noam Chomsky, writers like Howard Zinn, even Gore Vidal—writers like that, who had a sort of dissident view of U.S. military force abroad and at home.

And so, I just became critical of the power structures in this country. Basically [those who] oppress and suppress organic democratic movements, whether that's labor unions or civil rights movements, anyone that questions the established centers of power in this country, which I came to see as largely affiliated with concentrations of corporate power and concentrations of money—a kind of oligarchy, if you will, or 'corporate oligarchy.'

And that has basically defined how I have viewed politics ever since; and sometimes [I admire] critiques that are aligned with forces on the Left, and sometimes I affiliate with some critics that come out on the Right—especially against centralized power. I think the Right is more critical of centralized power in the government. I also, as we've talked about before, see concentrations of power by corporations and oligarchs as a big problem. But I view all of those as huge issues.

ME: Do you feel that protesting is an effective mechanism for enacting meaningful change?

KEVIN: Yeah, I do. I don't think it's the only thing. I think when people talk about theories of change, there's the kind of "inside / outside forces." The outside forces might be protesters who are marching the streets, who are demonstrating to the establishment forces—the *body politic* in Washington DC or other centers of power in this country—that there's genuine movement and popular discontent over a policy or popular support for certain policies.

We know that, for example, the *March on Washington* that Martin Luther King was part of in the early 1960s is well known and famous. But I think it's less well known that the Civil Rights Movement had been threatening to march in Washington since the Second World War, led by people like A. Philip Randolph, who came up through the union movement through the *Brotherhood of the Sleeping Car Porters*, and it was actually they [who] were threatening FDR at the beginning of the Second World War. They wanted to desegregate federal contracting in the defense industry for the war effort, and they threatened that if he didn't act on that, they would march on Washington. And Roosevelt just didn't want to deal with the repercussions of that, so he did issue an executive order that gave into some of their demands.

And so that's an example right there of how a protest movement has affected policy. And one can talk about the impacts of protests of Vietnam, [or] on apartheid South Africa, for example, the US support for apartheid South Africa—that sort of thing. So, I do think it [protesting] has its role, but it's not the end-all-be-all.

ME: Do you mind explaining what brought you to the Occupy Wall Street movement and what your role was during those protests?

KEVIN: I was living in Boston, and I was working at an environmental NGO. Again, I had come years before to become very critical of corporate power and the impact that corporate power had on the federal government—which especially seemed very corrupt during the George W. Bush years. But you also kind of saw that with the Obama administration that came into power in early 2009 that took a much more corporate friendly approach than I think a lot of people had expected.

So, [I witnessed] the 2008 financial crisis and the recession it caused and all the deep economic harm that caused. And then we saw the banks getting bailed out by the federal government under a program that had been started by the George W. Bush administration and then carried out by the Obama administration. And we saw millions and millions of people losing their homes. And millions—tens of millions— of people out of work and not getting the kind of support that the banks were getting. And a lot of the people who were directly involved in a lot of the illegal activity that led to the financial collapse got off scot-free while, again, millions of working Americans suffered!

So, around the fall of 2011 I was living in Boston. The *Occupy Wall Street* movement had started in New York City (hence the name). But then it inspired protests all around the country and other *Occupy* movements. You know: "Occupy Washington, DC," "Occupy Seattle" — and the form that it took was encampments, some strategically placed places around different cities.

So, there was one that started in Boston—I think it was around September 2011—right in a place called Dewey

Square. For those who know Boston, that's right in front of South Station; it's right near the beginning of the financial district of Boston. It's right across the street from the Federal Reserve.

And they set up an encampment. I was not there on the first day. It was a couple weeks into it that I actually went, and I went just as an observer initially, just walking around and talking to the different people who were there to understand why they were there. And there are a lot of different reasons why different people were there.

But I found it fascinating! And having studied a lot of different social movements and social protest movements that had sprung up not just in the United States but in different countries around the world, I was really impressed and really interested and wanted to be a part of it.

So, I just started talking to people about how one can get involved and volunteer. And before I knew it, I was there every day for the next couple of months. Sometimes I slept there in tents and kind of became part of the movement!

ME: Do you feel that after these protests your demands were met and concessions made by the Big Banks? Or do you feel that the movement, more or less, fizzled out?

KEVIN: So, there were no specific demands that were made. A big critique that the corporate media and many people expressed at the time was there's not a list of demands that *Occupy Wall Street* or any of these occupy movements are making.

I do think there were probably a few things here and there, like 'break up the banks,' but there was no formal statement. Part of that had to do with the makeup of the Occupy movements, and I can only speak to *Occupy Boston* because that's the one that I was involved in. But there is a real effort to ingrain anarchic principles. There is this whole thing of having... I think it was called "horizontal organization" or something like that, but basically not trying to have any kind of a hierarchy. And that led to not having a formal structure that could issue demands.

There was also such a diversity of opinions. There were people that were straight up anarchist who wanted to abolish the government. There were people who wanted some small reforms. There were those who were self-avowed communists and socialists. There were also people who were explicitly libertarian; they detested communism. But we all had the critique of the banks and the federal government in common.

So, there was no conscious decision to issue any specific demands, and I should say we did have an organizational body; it was called 'The General Assembly', which was kind of a Parliament kind of thing. There were no elected representatives, but you would meet every day at I think it was five o'clock. Anyone who wanted [could] go and you would elect what was called a facilitator—basically someone to kind of run the show.

You would vote on an agenda and then you could pass various resolutions and so there would be a resolution condemning something the government was doing. But there were no explicit demands that were being made. And I always thought that was fine with me because I viewed it more as an expression of popular discontent. And, again, going back to what I was speaking about earlier, I thought it was a demonstration of this idea that there was a large movement that was disaffected with what was going on in Washington, DC and other halls of power in this country, and that the government—or whomever—could see that, and then perhaps people with explicit policy ideas or people coming out of academia or think tanks could take that and develop it into specific policies that could be carried out knowing that there is popular energy behind it.

And I would argue that you DID see some of that come out. Years later, I think that provided the foundation for things like the rise of Bernie Sanders, who was still a US senator at that time, but he had not started to run for President yet. You saw around that time that Elizabeth Warren had just been elected and she started connecting herself to that and pushing for policies that were hugely critical of corporate power.

You started to see the beginnings of the development of corporate critiques on the Right as well. Which you later saw come out with people like JD Vance or Josh Hawley. So, it's hard to trace it all directly back to the Occupy movement. But I do think it provided a lot of that foundation and then you have to wonder where everyone kind of went today.

A lot of people went into positions on Capitol Hill supporting Ro Khanna or Bernie Sanders working for them. Or I think you saw some of the energy go into organizations like *Justice Democrats*, which then supported candidates like Alexandria Ocasio-Cortez, and so I think it provided a lot of energy—it almost incubated the movement that became the "Sanders' wing" of the Democratic Party, which was economic populist. Not, I would argue, not quite "woke." I think there's a development that happened later that caused that, but that class-based critique of the way things were run in this country.

And I think if you did not have the Occupy movement, I would question whether Sanders [would have] had that success or if we would have seen the success of a lot of those left-wing candidates who came into positions of power later.

ME: So, what I'm hearing you say is that the *Occupy* movement essentially planted seeds to what would become a much larger and more successful action-based critique of the Big Banks and other institutional power structures. Is that a fair assessment?

KEVIN: Yeah. I think that's a great metaphor. I think it planted seeds and fertilized the ground and then we saw different things spring up from there.

ME: Ok, so since you were there with "boots on the ground" (and a tent in the dirt), I am hoping you can validate something for me. In this chapter I make the point that "woke" alignment by the Big Banks started to manifest with suspicious timing around the Occupy Wallstreet timeline.

And frankly not just the Big Banks; the *Military Industrial Complex*, which you mentioned earlier, starts "going woke" not long after this. For example, one begins seeing Lockheed Martin and Raytheon begin implementing DEI programs and flying rainbow flags to deflect from the fact the US Government is dropping their bombs on women and children. But, going back to the Big Banks for a second, do you feel that this pivot worked in any way, shape, or form to deflect some of the criticism it was facing? Was the spotlight turned off the banking sector by the Progressive Left after it became "woke"?

KEVIN: Yeah, I think it's intentionally done. Yes, by the banks and all those companies. And I think there's an interesting book that I read last year by Ryan Grim, which talks about this. It's hard to quite pinpoint the moment when this happened. But [his book] gets into the 2016 Primary campaign on the Democratic side between Bernie Sanders and Hillary Clinton.

And again, Bernie Sanders was very economic-populist and critical of Wall Street—critical of the military industrial complex. All that, but not really leaning into racial issues or, you know, LGBT issues or any of that. I mean, he was always on the Left, but he wasn't leaning into any of that.

Ryan Grim talks about how the Clinton campaign, which is very closely allied with Wall Street, saw Bernie Sanders as a real threat. And I think all the donors and the establishment forces within the party were really concerned because it looked for a while there that Bernie Sanders could actually take the nomination away from her. And there is a conscious decision to attack Bernie Sanders not from the economic left—but to start painting him as a *racist*—or at least someone who didn't care about issues of systemic racism or the rights of LGBT people or anything like that.

There's a great quote from Hillary Clinton at this time where she's making a speech and she says, "you know, we could break up the big banks tomorrow, but that won't solve systemic racism." Suggesting that that's the real ill of our society.

This is also the time when we started hearing "Bernie Bros" used as a kind of pejorative term—that there is this kind of toxic masculinity within the Sanders campaign of largely men, and the Clinton people explicitly say "largely white men who are exhibiting toxic masculinity" having disdain for issues like the *Black Lives Matter* movement (which had started) and other important social issues.

And she used that over and over again to kind of beat him down. And her campaign obviously went down in defeat after she got the nomination. But I think a lot of the seeds that she had planted there slowly started to take over the party.

A lot of these large corporations saw that it was successful in beating back Bernie Sanders. And I think they thought "well, this is a successful way to kind of de-fang the movement. If we could cloak ourselves in these woke issues and start talking about systemic racism, embracing DEI, putting up rainbow flags in front of our offices, then that will take a lot of the energy out. We can kind of divide the movement because a lot of people on the Left who support Bernie Sanders may also think that systemic racism is [more] important."

So, when you create these cleavages, you're able to divide and conquer, and you put the real economic populace in the corner as this "toxic, racist people" and then the real "heroes" are the banks and the defense contractors who have those rainbow flags and those DEI programs. So, again, that's Ryan Grim's formulation. I think there's a lot of merit to that and it makes sense to me that a lot of that stemmed from that 2016 primary campaign.

ME: I liked your term "de-fanged." Have the Big Banks effectively de-fanged the critiques of them by clothing themselves in woke propaganda or woke ideology?

KEVIN: Well, I think you're partially right. But I think it's very easy for us to almost make it sound like there were "evil intentions." And I do think screwing people out of their homes through criminal activities or bombing wedding parties in Pakistan and making millions of dollars off of it *is* evil.

But I would also say, as someone who works with many companies, I think the people who do that are fully "bought into" the kind of woke ideology and maybe we're getting too far into human psychology here, but it might be a way of them convincing themselves that there's a kind of righteous mission that they're working on.

And, so, while they're making bombs that go kill people, I do think they're really believing that they are fulfilling the legacy of Martin Luther King and suffragettes and Stonewall and all that.

And, so, I think they feel really good about putting that flag up and they're not, I guess – to sort of mix metaphors – they're not quite "twirling their mustaches." They go to bed at night thinking "I'm making very positive change for this world."

I think what they are actually doing – and what it sounds like we both agree on – is they've deluded themselves into thinking that they're doing good for the world when they're actually doing a lot of harm. But I would say everyone involved in this story thinks that they're doing the right thing and it's rushing to judge whether they are or not. And, again, I think we kind of both agree that they're not.

ME: Good point. Maybe I used a poor analogy suggesting that they think themselves evil or that they are evil.

I think you're completely right. What is happening is that "the road to hell is being paved with good intentions," and they may be attempting to sooth themselves with a balm. They believe themselves good people and righteous and doing the right thing for trying to solve humanity's racism problem and all other "isms." But they are blinding themselves to the errors and machinations of their own actions. And again, when you go back to military industrial complex, it's easy to see how when you bomb a civilian family BUT you did it with a "Trans Rights" sticker on your bomb, that doesn't make it any more righteous.

As for the banking sector, Big Bank bailouts and Federal Reserve policies are essentially bankrupting the middle class, inflating the dollar, enriching billionaires, and making the American poor even poorer than ever before. BUT, damn, do they have a terrific DEI program! Yet I would contend this doesn't wash away all manner of sins. Not by a mile.

How can we find a solution that allows these corporations to take a hard look in the mirror and make real, meaningful change in their organizations?

KEVIN: How can corporations change themselves into doing that? Well, this is where we might differ. Because I think this is all just a product of capitalism.

If you're Lockheed Martin, your *raison d'être* is to make money – to maximize profits for your shareholders. And you're following the logic of that structure and embracing these movements and these flags because it allows you to shield yourself from more criticism and thus it allows you to get more contracts and make more money for your shareholders. So, I don't think they'll just change on their own because they're not moral agents.

We are starting to see a push back on things like embracing DEI and those initiatives from corporations because of pushback from the Right (people like Chris Ruffo). This stems from concern that corporations have embraced "woke liberal ideology" and they were all anti-Trump. That sort of thing.

So, we are starting to see some of it roll back, but it is interesting that it's coming from the Right.

I'm just amazed by aspects of the Left that basically buy this bullshit—like *you've been fooled by companies just putting up a flag!?!* And it makes you wonder why they were critical of those companies in the first place.

So, I think if there was change that it would come from the Left. It would be from that kind of old school economic populist left that I had always affiliated myself with—that kind of "Sanders' wing" of the party, from building up a stronger base and building up allies and organizing based on a critique of corporate power as a dominant theme in that critique. And so, you'd be less susceptible to being fooled by a flag going up in front of the Lockheed Martin offices and [believing] they're great because they are embracing these programs.

But I think it takes a lot of education and organizing coming from that aspect of the Left…

Because—I should say, that's who the audience is, right?

Like for Lockheed Martin or the big banks – when they are doing this—when they're embracing woke values, it's not to assuage people on the Right! It's not. Their audience is not Republicans or conservatives or people in the Tea Party. The entire point of it is to address the audience of the Left, and they've been largely successful, I think.

But it's really only half the country and that's something that they have to battle with.

ME: Kevin, thank you so much for your viewpoints. As always, you're brilliant and articulate and everything that most people should aspire to be. I appreciate your wisdom.

KEVIN: I just wish I could give more.

"Whenever you find yourself on the side of the majority, it is time to pause and reflect."
*— **Mark Twain***

CASE IN POINT: WOKE HYSTERIA

As illustrated in previous chapters, Wokeism is often hard to properly describe or objectively criticize because of its over-reaching (and ever-changing) definition(s). "Woke" has to carry a lot of water for the Left because it has become such an over-generalized term for "everything Progressive." As such, let's look at a handful of examples which serve as meaningful manifestations, in and of themselves, why a *Metamodern deconstruction* and critique of Wokeism is appropriate to move forward and reach a new paradigm that is more efficacious.

Corrupted Language

George Orwell once wrote:

> *"But if thought corrupts language, language can also corrupt thought."* (Orwell, "1984")

This axiom highlights the dangers of using vague or manipulative language; doing so often restricts critical thinking and understanding. Orwell accurately assesses the self-evident and reciprocal relationship between language and thought, suggesting that imprecise language will shape and limit how people perceive and engage with the world. In contemporary society, debates over terminology—such as pronouns, identity labels, or redefined terms for common words like "exercise" or "overweight"—illustrate how language changes can influence collective thinking, sometimes fostering greater inclusivity but also creating deep ideological divides. Orwell's warning begs us to approach language with critical awareness, ensuring it reflects truth and clarity rather than serving as a political *tool* for controlling thought or stifling dissent.

I bring this up to highlight the dangers of Woke culture using intentionally obscure and convoluted words, phrases, idioms, or other language all the in the name of "protecting" one's delicate sensibilities and/or to avoid offending.

Here is one example. My sister-in-law visited her medical practitioner in Vermont earlier this month. She was asked to fill out a short form as part of the administrative check-in process. One of the health questions read "How Often Do You Joyfully Move Your Body?"

My sister did a double-take and had to consider the question for a minute. *Joyfully move my body?* With careful reflection, she finally realized this must be an overly complex new euphemism meant to replace the simple and unambiguous word "exercise." Once she figured that out, she was able to answer the question.

Yet the obvious concern now becomes: why did language for a simple medical onboarding questionnaire need to be so altered as to make it unnecessarily convoluted and esoteric? Why was it changed? Well, for seemingly good intentions: to protect an extremely small subset of persons who might conceivably be offended by the word "exercise."

For to properly *speak in tongues* of the Church of Wokeism, this modification to the language was exercised (no pun intended) because "it frames physical activity in an *inclusive way*, reducing *mental and emotional anxiety* some may associate with *harmful rhetoric* when using the word 'exercise'—which is known to have a *negative connotation* or *triggering* effect."

However, let's consider a few reasonable counter points to these kinds of arguments. For starters, changing language is especially harmful to those who leverage English as a second language. Imagine an immigrant to this country attempting to read and decipher important medical questions on the form. "Joyful movement of the body" is not a recognizable term in English, much less in another world language.

Secondly, let's consider other negative externalities of this revision. At best, this change in vernacular will invariably create bloat and inefficiencies in the patient onboarding process; at worst, it may serve to make the staff or practitioners at the medical office appear to be "a joke." This is a particularly dangerous outcome if it increases the likelihood of patients in need of important care to be distrustful of their doctors' medical advice. The presence of nonsensical "woke" jargon may potentially discolor the value of medical prognoses or prescriptions provided. Certain patients may leave their doctor's office asking themselves, "Why would I listen to that quack's advice when he's obviously given into the *'woke mind virus*?'" This kind of thinking might cause them to "throw the baby out with the bathwater." In short, in this increasingly divided political climate, the **unintended consequences** for a medical facility simply trying to "prevent offending" its patients, may ironically cause more harm than good through the application of nonsensical jargon. Such practices create a self-inflicted wound and serve only to perpetuate a mad race to the bottom.

War on Words

The anecdote just described is certainly not all-inclusive of the silliness that occurs with respect to the bastardization of language. In addition to the political "War on Drugs," "War on Terror," and "War on Poverty," a variable Postmodern "War on Words" might be in the making—with the Progressive Left initiating a comprehensive set of preemptive strikes over the last several years. Specifically, the proliferation of new words, new phrases, and new idioms have entered the cultural zeitgeist with reckless abandon. Here are just a few examples worth noting:

(1) Phrases like "human milk" or "chest-feeding" are replacing "breastfeeding" to be more inclusive of non-binary or transgender parents.
(2) "Menstruators" is now used instead of "women" or "girls." This term includes *all* people who menstruate, regardless of gender identity, such as transgender men and non-binary individuals.
(3) The term "pregnant people" is used instead of "pregnant women" to acknowledge that not all individuals who can give birth identify as female.

(4) The term "homeless person" has been replaced with "unhoused" or "person experiencing homelessness" to focus on the individual rather than their condition.

(5) "Mother" has been replaced with "birthing parent" in certain medical or legal contexts.

(6) "Bodies with vaginas" instead of "women" has been used to ensure inclusivity for transgender and non-binary individuals who may not identify as women but have the anatomy referenced.

(7) "Historymakers" instead of "forefathers" is the new gender-neutral term because it avoids male-centric language.

(8) Similarly, "Snowperson" is now recommended instead of "snowman."

(9) In an effort to replace an already replaced word, "Global Majority" now is recommended to be used to replace "people of color" (which itself was created to replace other racial terms).

(10) "Parenting Partner" is recommended to replace "mother" or "father." This new term is used to describe parents without assigning traditional gender roles, focusing on the partnership dynamic rather than biological or gendered distinctions.

(11) A new "ism" has been created in the last few years; "Speciesism" now describes prejudice against non-human animals. This term was coined to challenge the idea that humans are inherently superior to animals, often used in discussions about veganism and animal rights.

(12) "Lived Experience" now serves as a stand-in for "anecdotal evidence."

As might be expected, critics of the Postmodern framework argue that such terms are imprecise, ambiguous, excessive, or confusing, creating unnecessary complexity in language. Critics also point out the "silliness" of being offended by words which we all know and have used for many hundreds of years. However, practitioners of the *Church of Wokeism* view such terms as components in their spiritual lexicon and critical tools to foster inclusivity and respect.

Legal Challenges

Examples abound of shifting language causing challenges in day-to-day life. Some daycares reportedly have begun listing "people caring for children" instead of "parents" on forms, leaving grandparents and nannies wondering if these terms apply to them. Other instances occur in corporate workplaces where new "equity-focused" policies refer to employees as "members of our collaborative ecosystem," leading to puzzled reactions about the chain of command. Similarly, a city council recently labeled garbage collectors as "sanitation heroes," causing confusion when multiple residents sought to confirm trash pickup schedules.

Adding ambiguity to language can also cause significant harm, specifically when precision in language is critical, such as in legal or medical contexts. For example, in custody disputes, "woke" language such as "non-birthing parent" has created confusion regarding parental roles and rights. For instance, cases involving same-sex couples or situations where the biological and gestational roles differ often highlight the term's limitations. One notable case involved a dispute between a biological parent and a "non-birthing partner" over custody and parental responsibilities, which led to extended litigation due to unclear terminology and legal recognition of parenthood. Prolonged court proceedings, expert testimonies, and the need for appeals can result in legal fees exceeding tens of thousands of dollars, burdening families and complicating the lives of the children involved.

Speaking of legal challenges, multiple lawsuits have been filed related to *Diversity, Equity, and Inclusion* (DEI) programs. For example, in 2023 no fewer than thirty-seven (37) federal lawsuits challenging DEI initiatives were filed in the U.S., up from eleven (11) in 2021. These cases often allege constitutional violations, with some high-profile lawsuits, such as *Duvall v. Novant Health*, leading to multimillion-dollar damages. Such cases often stem from ambiguity in the language used in policies and training, which can result in misinterpretation or allegations of bias.

Companies implementing DEI programs have faced formal accusations alleging reverse discrimination, with plaintiffs arguing that these "Woke" initiatives unfairly disadvantage certain demographic groups, particularly white employees or men. Multiple lawsuits have been filed against employers for using terms like "systemic privilege" or emphasizing "equity of outcomes" in ways that plaintiffs claim create a hostile work environment or violate anti-discrimination laws. Such cases often focus on whether DEI programs, as implemented, cross the line into legally prohibited forms of discrimination

Another issue arises when ambiguous language from the *Church of Wokeism*'s DEI initiatives causes confusion around implementation or compliance. For instance, companies might outline vague goals like "achieving equity," leaving employees unclear on how success is measured or what actions are required. Ambiguities can lead to inconsistent enforcement or accusations of favoritism, sparking legal disputes. Financially, defending these cases can cost hundreds of thousands of dollars, particularly when they involve protracted litigation, reputational harm, or the need to revise corporate policies to align with clearer legal standards.

Many of these aforementioned examples are emblematic of potentially dangerous shifting goalposts and an alarming propensity for the Postmodern era to morph directed language into muted or politically sensitive language. Sadly, this cultural disposition only makes our world less colorful and more restricted. We wind up talking much but saying little. We sacrifice precision, or even veracity, on the altar of politeness.

Society has been gravitating towards a proverbial **"*euphemism treadmill*,"** which is a term first coined by Steven Pinker. This effect refers to the phenomenon where words initially used to be polite or "politically correct" soon become associated with negative connotations, forcing people to constantly invent new, less offensive terms to replace them, creating a *continuous cycle of replacing words* that have become stigmatized—essentially, a "treadmill" of needing to find new euphemisms as old ones become 'negative.'

> "POLITICAL LANGUAGE — AND WITH VARIATIONS THIS IS TRUE OF ALL POLITICAL PARTIES, FROM CONSERVATIVES TO ANARCHISTS — IS DESIGNED TO MAKE LIES SOUND TRUTHFUL AND TO GIVE AN APPEARANCE OF SOLIDITY TO PURE WIND."
> —GEORGE ORWELL

An Appeal to Common Sense?

It sometimes seems necessary to shout into the wind, "*Are we all taking crazy pills, people?!?*"

There is no rational reason to relabel the term "exercise" to "joyful moving of the body." Exercise is a succinct, clear, and perfectly useful term to explain physical activity. That some super small minority of people might possibly take offense to the word (or be "triggered" by it) should not be a catalyst for shifting our entire language to the left. There should exist a higher bar for words or phrases to morph.

The backlash to what many see as sheer absurdity is understandable and defensible. The Progressive Left *speaking in tongues* of the Woke—and specifically the act of forcing that language on non-practitioners—may cause a similar level of media backlash that the Pentecostal Church has faced from within and without its ranks. Religious Faith and using the lexicon of the Church is one thing, but blind faith and ungrounded vocal hysteria is something completely different.

WOKE BLOWBACK & WOKE REVULSION

The term *Woke* has become toxic to many Americans. This is just a fact. Even if one fully embraces the merits of the ideology—including standing up to prejudice and power imbalances—the term simply no longer is a good standard-bearer for the Progressive movement. The well has become polluted. The word carries too much baggage.

One may blame the Right for this. Opponents on the conservative side let fly the word "woke" from their lips with it dripping with righteous disdain. Yet the Left should consider taking a long, hard look at its own dogma when reflecting on the cultural divide.

Did the Progressive Left "spike the football" in the era of rampant Postmodern thought instead of allowing nuance and civil discourse to take place? Many on the Right feel strongly that the *Church of Wokeism has* poured hot bile down its throat for more than a decade. From this perspective, the heretical countermovement to Wokeism and its Holy Doctrine is mostly the making of the Progressive Left.

The Left often blames "the resurgence of racism" largely

on Donald Trump. But consider that the rise of Trump, as a populist movement, was directly because of the self-righteous zeal coming from *The Church of Wokeism*. Postmodern America has been facing movements and counter movements, actions and reciprocal actions. The pendulum has swung far to the Left—and then swings back even harder to the Right. Back and forth, back and forth. This deadly dance and grueling game of political machinations does little to evolve the cultural wellbeing of our country. A little humility is in order; some temperance and acceptance of the other side would go a long way – instead of touchdown celebrations and constantly forcing "your enemy" to eat humble pie.

Consider this example from recent memory. Gay and homosexual rights in America gained momentum and acceptance through decades of activism, cultural shifts, and legal victories. Landmark moments, such as the *Stonewall Riots* in 1969, catalyzed the modern LGBTQ+ movement, while increasing visibility in media and the work of advocacy groups normalized LGBTQ+ identities. Legal milestones like the repeal of "Don't Ask, Don't Tell" and the Supreme Court's 2015 decision to legalize same-sex marriage reflected and furthered public acceptance.

These were extremely positive results for the Progressive movement from this time period; increased social acceptance and legal protections for gay individuals resulted in mass acceptance and a reduction in discrimination. And this all happened well before "Woke" was even in the public lexicon! In fact, mass support for gay and lesbian rights, including same-sex marriage, significantly increased over the decades leading up to modern-day Wokeism. According to *Gallup* in

2016, around 62% of Americans supported same-sex marriage (up from 36% ten years earlier), reflecting broad acceptance across many demographics.

Today, more than **90% of Americans** support the right of gay, lesbian, and bisexual individuals to live as freely as they choose. This strong support includes backing for nondiscrimination protections, with majorities across political, religious, and ethnic lines favoring these rights. For instance, a 2023 poll highlighted that two-thirds of Republicans, 82% of independents, and 90% of Democrats endorse nondiscrimination protections for LGBTQ+ individuals. Among religious groups, support also remains high, with more than three-quarters of white Catholics, Black Protestants, and other major denominations supporting these rights.

All-in-all, the LGBTQA+ movement has experienced tremendous momentum and acceptance in a short period of time (again, the vast majority of this support coming PRIOR to the Woke movement). However, instead of taking the "W," the envelope was pushed by the *Church of Wokeism*! In recent years, the Woke Left has attempted a "bridge too far" by pushing "gender affirming care" for children under the age of eighteen. This massive overreach woke up a sleeping bear as the countermovement pushed back.

Gender Affirming Care

The LGBTQ+ movement's broad embrace of gender-affirming care for minors began gaining significant momentum in the mid-2010s, with organizations like the *World Professional Association for Transgender Health* (WPATH) and *The Trevor Project* supporting such programs. A large number of critics of these programs openly decried them as "child abuse" and "child mutilation." Despite this pushback, by 2015 public and professional advocacy for medical interventions like puberty blockers and hormone therapy had solidified as part of the standard framework for addressing gender dysphoria in abused and/or confused youth. This advocacy coincided with a growing focus on mental health and the recognition of the high risks of depression and suicidality in gender-confused adolescents when care was inaccessible.

By the late 2010s, the focus shifted to legislation and public awareness, with major medical organizations like the *American Academy of Pediatrics* endorsing gender-affirming care as "safe and beneficial" when carefully managed. This shift was bolstered by certain research apparently claiming improved mental health outcomes, such as reduced depression and suicidal ideation when minors were supported in their "preferred gender identity" through both social and medical transitions. Parental involvement and mental health assessments were emphasized as critical components of this care model.

The pushback on these programs intensified on the Right. Child advocacy groups spoke out for the children they perceived were being abused or misguided by exigent pressures. However, the Woke Left's emphasis on gender-affirming care continued to grow, particularly in response to increasing legislative efforts to restrict such care in the early 2020s. These controversial efforts sparked further advocacy from certain LGBTQ+ organizations and medical professionals, who underscored the ethical and medical necessity of providing supportive and evidence-based care to minors who were instructed or otherwise led to believe they were "born in the wrong body."

As a result of these efforts, there has continued to be a rising and substantial pushback to gender-affirming care, particularly for minors ("child abuse" as such treatments are referred to on the Right). Opposition comes from a variety of political, social, and medical perspectives and has intensified in recent years. Critics often raise concerns about the ethical, medical, and social implications of such care. These critics, including *detransitioners*, argue that puberty blockers, hormones, and surgeries carry significant risks such as long-term health impacts, reduced fertility, and insufficiently informed consent from minors.

Legislative efforts in over 20 states have sought to ban such treatments, framing it as a measure to protect children from irreversible decisions. Cultural and religious groups often oppose these treatments based on traditional beliefs about gender and concerns over rising rates of gender dysphoria diagnoses.

According to polling data, the percentage of Americans who favor healthcare professionals providing medical gender-transition treatments to those under the age of eighteen is well below 33%. The majority consensus on the topic of "gender affirming care" for minors is that other terms are more medically and morally accurate, such as "experimental treatments on children" and "irreversible medical procedures."

The point here is that the Woke Left, of their own volition, chose to discolor a relatively healthy, popular, accepted, and vibrant social movement (the LGBTQA+ organization), by tarnishing it with a wildly unpopular sortie on innocent children. This was "spiking the football" in the endzone at a time when humility and respect for differing viewpoints was in order.

As an outcome of this hard push by the Woke Left's advocacy of "gender-affirming care" (aka "irreversible medical procedures") for minors, data suggests that national support for the LGTBQA+ community has shifted significantly—and has even fractured the movement from the inside out. For example, the following groups have formed in recent years to combat attempts to stunt or medically impact the natural development of children:

- **Gays Against Groomers** is a group of LGBTQ+ individuals formed in 2022 that opposes the sexualization of children and the promotion of gender-affirming treatments for minors, asserting that such practices are harmful and should be restricted. The organization focuses on advocating for children's safety and privacy, especially in schools, while drawing attention to what it sees as ideological overreach in medical and educational systems.

- **Trans Against Groomers** is a partner group of *Gays Against Groomers*, composed of conservative transgender individuals and *detransitioners* who oppose gender-affirming care for minors.

- **Our Duty** is an international organization that focuses on opposing gender transitions for minors. It is comprised of parents and others concerned about what they view as the risks of early medical interventions for children identifying as transgender.

- **Parents Defending Education**, though not exclusively focused on LGBTQ+ issues, addresses concerns about educational policies they see as promoting ideological indoctrination, including discussions around gender identity in schools.

- **Protect Women's Sports** is a group advocating for policies that limit transgender women's participation in women's sports. While not directly opposing gender-affirming care, its advocacy intersects with broader debates on gender identity.

These specific groups emerge from a wide array of differing ideological and personal perspectives, ranging from concerns about child welfare and parental rights to broader cultural or political objections. Their activities have sparked significant controversy, drawing proverbial "fire and brimstone" ire from the bully-pulpit of the *Church of Wokeism*.

As described thoroughly, *The Church* celebrates diversity and inclusion with gusto, but not diversity of viewpoint on faith-based topics it deems righteous and unassailable.

Woke Irony

The sad irony of Wokeism is that its concerted efforts to cast a spotlight on injustice and improve the world may backfire and only serve to make society more divided. This is not a criticism of its motives, but its *methods*. Like a Pentecostal preacher, The Woke have sought to use the bully-pulpit to affect change and bifurcate believers from unbelievers. But this modality is crude, ineffective, and often violently misfires.

The current reality is that the *Church of Wokeism* is turning off more people than it is converting. The "fire and brimstone" sermons are losing their desired effect. The "sexist and/or racist wolf" has been cried too many times. As a result, followers are turning away from Wokeism and running in the opposite direction.

The Left might argue that the Right is turning to racism as an overreaction to Woke Culture. They would point to the rise of Trump/MAGA as an example. Whether or not this is an accurate criticism remains to be seen. But the point is a valid one. Has the wild and intelligible screaming by frenzied Woke preachers in the sacred halls of the *Church of Wokeism* boomeranged? Because of Wokeism, has the Right galvanized its base and found its own righteous cause to rally behind?

If this is the case, the Church has no one to blame but itself. Temperance might have been a wiser course of action than blood conquest. But just as in any Holy War, when dividing lines are starkly drawn, and one's faith is *righteous,* there is a "take no prisoners" attitude—you're either with us or you're against us. The faithful will live in Woke heaven; the unfaithful will perish in Conservative hell.

And when the political rhetoric is this divisive, as can truly occur only in religious affectations, then there can be no mercy. It's kill or be killed—do or die—become Woke or become the enemy. And the great irony is that the scourge of Wokeism may die by its own self-righteous sword.

"He who joyfully marches to music in rank and file has already earned my contempt. He has been given a large brain by mistake, since for him the spinal cord would suffice."
— **Albert Einstein**

THE WOKE RIGHT

"Do not repay anyone evil for evil."
Romans 12:17

"Do not fight evil with evil or insult with insult."
1 Peter 3:9

Before we can dive into what metamodern *dialectical synthesis* looks like in the current era (i.e. our "target state" for the cultural evolution of Wokeism), we must first explore what it plainly is NOT. In the Right's kneejerk reaction to the Woke Left, it has strangely developed its own brand of Wokeism. While a full-blown "church planting" has not quite taken root, in many ways, this is the Right's method of "fighting fire with fire."

The term "The Woke Right" started to gain traction around 2019. It was during this period that analysts began to observe and label a shift in certain conservative circles, where identity politics—typically a hallmark of the Left—was being increasingly used by some on the Right to argue against Progressive viewpoints.

In this way, the conservative movement essentially co-opted elements of identity politics and Wokeism (which itself was derived from a word that was co-opted from the Black

Rights movement), to advance its own agenda.

A prominent example of this dynamic is the use of identity politics in the defense of Israel, particularly in the context of the Israeli-Palestinian conflict. The Woke Right has framed its support for Israel as "a defense of Jewish identity and survival," invoking historical narratives of Jewish victimhood and persecution, such as the Holocaust, to justify Israel's actions. This rhetorical strategy is used to counter the Left's candid critique of Israeli policies, particularly regarding the bombing campaigns in Gaza and the unfair treatment of Palestinians. By framing any legitimate criticism of the State of Israel as inherently anti-Semitic, the Woke Right uses identity politics to position themselves as the "defenders of Jewish people" against what they claim to perceive as a growing tide of anti-Israel sentiment on the Left.

To elaborate on this point and to demonstrate an amusing case of irony, Dave Smith and Robert Bernstein, two **Jewish** hosts of the political podcast, "Part of the Problem," have both been labeled "antisemitic" due to their public condemnation of Israel's bombing campaign of Gaza. Their critics come from the "Woke Right" persuasion. In response to specific opprobrium, Dave Smith provided the following response on his podcast:

> "[…] Second of all, when do we ever 'rant about the Jews'? We're a show hosted by two Jews! We've never expressed hostility or anything [of the kind] toward Jewish people.
>
> I am a critic of the *government of Israel*! So, you're conflating criticizing a government policy with being a bigot. Oh, wait a minute, hold on. So, I somehow lose my Jewishness…? I'm not really a Jew now

because I don't have the 'right political opinions?' Hmm, who does that remind you of? Who criticizes black conservatives that way and calls them Uncle Toms and says, you're not really black anymore? Who? You know who I mean? It's the Joe Biden. 'If you don't vote for me, you're not black.'

[...] I'm going to give you two views, and you tell me how it is possible to not see the contradiction in these two views, okay? Here are the two views, Rob:

I am opposed to identity politics. That's view number one. Number two, *I support Zionism.*

Tell me how you can *possibly* hold those two views and not see the obvious contradiction? 'I believe in a government for a particular identity group, but I oppose identity politics.'

Zionism is the *definition* of identity politics!

And listen, I'll say this, I've never been a guy who really rants against identity politics because it's kind of a slippery definition and there could be some identity politics that I would have absolutely no problem with. I'll give you an example: Maj Toure. He runs a group called *Black Guns Matter.* I have no problem with that whatsoever. It is clearly *identitarian.* He's talking about how there's been kind of like a racist history behind gun control legislation and that it's often black people who are in these high crime areas, the law-abiding Black people who need the Second Amendment the most. Now, that is identitarian, but it's also just fighting for gun rights and for getting government out of the way of people's right to defend themselves. So, I have no problem with that at all.

And I don't even, in theory, have a problem with Zionism. I don't have a problem if there's a group of Jewish people who want to start a society together and they want it to be explicitly for Jewish people. I'd have no problem with that.

Listen, if Jews had, say, purchased the land legitimately from Arabs and not violated the natural rights of the Arab population there, I wouldn't really have a problem with that. However, if you're going to support Zionism, don't give me this BS about how you're against identity politics!"

(Part Of The Problem: A Response to James Lindsay, Nov 27, 2024)

Another example of *Right Wokeism* is the use of identity politics around race, specifically in arguments about "reverse racism" and "woke culture." The Woke Right often frames itself as the defender of the rights of white working-class Americans, arguing that policies like affirmative action and diversity initiatives disproportionately favor racial minorities, leaving white individuals at a disadvantage.

These narratives echo traditional right-wing populism, but with an added focus on identity politics. They portray the Left's emphasis on racial equity as a form of discrimination against white people, framing it as an attack on their social and economic status. This strategy enables the *Woke Right* to engage in debates about race, framing themselves as the victims of Progressive racial justice agendas, and offering a counter-narrative that uses identity politics to align with working-class white Americans who feel sidelined by the modern Left's focus on minority rights.

The Woke Right Won't Cancel Out The Woke Left

What is clear by this escalation is that all the wrong lessons are being learned. Instead of opposing identity politics on the premise that they divide us, the Right has picked up the divisive weapons of the Left and is starting to use them for its own devices. This isn't *synthesis*, it's "eye for an eye" politics. It's regressive. And it's equally as absurd when the Right "goes Woke" as it is when the Left does (perhaps more so).

This is to say nothing about the incredible double standard at play! Selectively adopting elements of Progressive rhetoric while maintaining conservative principles comes across as insincere, inconsistent, and opportunistic. For this faction to use identity politics or cultural grievances as a way to advance traditionalist or nationalist agendas feels a bit like a monkey wearing human clothes. Instead of facing poor arguments head-on, employing merit and logic, the Woke Right has instead simply mirrored the doddering tactics of the Left—including cancel culture and moral outrage—while denouncing those exact same practices when they are used by Progressives. How sickeningly sanctimonious. How deliciously hypocritical!

Or as the Christian scriptures proclaim:

"Why do you look at the speck of sawdust in your brother's eye and pay no attention to the plank in your own eye? ... You hypocrite, first take the plank out of your own eye, and then you will see clearly to remove the speck from your brother's eye."
Matthew 7:3-5

A REASON FOR GREAT OPTIMISM

It has been my aim in these preceding chapters to put forth a premise and a narrative illustration of facts. The thesis is this: *Wokeism* is deeply rooted in the deconstructive Postmodern era—which, by definition, is cynical of established paradigms and thus aggressive to current power dynamics. The best virtue of Wokeism is its ability to challenge precepts involving power hierarchies which lead to hatred, prejudice, or oppression. In doing so, however, the complexities of the framework have been diluted and strayed far afield from hitting its target. This had led to *unintended consequences*—often at the expense of the very disenfranchised groups the framework aims to assist.

The cultural pendulum has shifted to the realm of the "absurd," with basic realities, simple axioms, and empirical facts now in the crossfire. In this era of Wokeism, identity politics now sits mainstage and often trumps reality. Compounding this, Wokeism has taken on so many priorities that the term now means nothing. In short, Woke has become a religion – and, like any religion, has succumbed to division, blind faith, and elitism by its dutiful practitioners.

We must move through and past Wokeism! We must

achieve *metamodern dialectical synthesis*. Our primary hope as a civilization is to evolve towards a new era that "moves beyond" Wokeism to a more complex framework that balances reality with cultural awareness and activism.

To get another perspective on this concluding point, I interviewed one of the great philosophical minds of our day with respect to developmental structuralism and the complexification of systems. He is a mainstay of reason and the published author of myriad books and papers on Metamodernism, transcendental thought, and the cultural evolution of meaning. He is my dear friend and brother, Brendan Dempsey.

Interview of Brendan Dempsey

ME: Brother, thank you so much for joining me today. I appreciate it. I would consider you an authority on the subject of Metamodernism and the various facets surrounding it. But I don't want my readers to take my word for it. I give you the floor; would you speak a bit to your bonafides? What brought you to this field of study and what are your published works on the topic?

BRENDAN: I discovered Metamodernism in 2013, not long after the seminal article, "Notes on Metamodernism" by Timotheus Vermeulen and Robin van den Akker was published. I discovered Metamodernism first in its cultural studies form, which at that point was still quite new and rather nascent. I'd gone looking for paradigms attempting to articulate what comes after Postmodernism—owing to my own discontent with the current options and aesthetic strategies on display by Postmodern cultural production.

It was in that context that I started asking, "Well, if there was a Modernism and a Postmodernism, is there a '*post-*

Postmodernism?'" That would have been in 2013 when I went searching for what literature there was talking about that prospect.

What Vermeulen and van den Akker were describing really spoke to me in a way that the Postmodern sensibility didn't. Postmodernism was a lot about deconstruction, problematization, a loss of meaning—a cynicism, a skepticism, all of which I experienced. But I didn't really find it satisfactory or sufficient for the kinds of work that I felt like the world really required, and that a meaningful life demanded.

And, so, what these Metamodern thinkers were saying as a response to the Postmodern moment really resonated. They were naming things like *a return of myth* and *informed naiveté* and *ironic sincerity*—and a kind of reconstructive mode which was very resonant with the things that I was doing in my own art and writing at the time. So, I got really excited about that, seeing that this could be some sort of emerging trend in culture that I could resonate with and really identify with.

I reached out to the authors of that article, who had then started a webzine called "Notes on Metamodernism" and I submitted a paper for their upcoming academic conference called *Oscillate! Metamodernism in the Humanities*, which they subsequently published.

ME: How many published articles and books have you written about this topic and what are some of the takeaways in that body of work that you can articulate?

BRENDAN: I went on to write a 7-volume series called *The Metamodern Spirituality Series*. I also have a podcast called *Metamodern Spirituality*. And most recently, and most importantly, I wrote a book in 2023 called

Metamodernism: Or, the Cultural Logic of Cultural Logics. One of the things that I tried to do in that is synthesize a lot of the strands of the Metamodern discourse that had appeared up until that point and tried to make a kind of comprehensive account of what structural aspects I saw.

ME: It's a good segue since you brought up synthesis. So, one of the thesis statements of my book is that the term (or philosophy around) 'Woke' essentially serves as an *archetype* for Postmodernism. What do you feel are "the goods, the bads, and the uglies" of that framework? How would you respond to that thesis? Do you believe it's accurate?

BRENDAN: Yeah, I think there's a lot to that. I think that the term "woke" best fits within a paradigmatically Postmodern shift, which is a turn towards recognitions of systems of socialization, systems of power, and the awareness of marginalization and oppressive dynamics that can be built into those systems. I think that the idea of "woke" then could be understood as a sort of popularized notion of more rarified academic discourse on similar topics as it emerged in the Academy to focus on critical examinations of racial, post-colonial, feminist, and queer kinds of analysis of culture and trying to shine a light on marginalized identities and marginalized sense-making structures within more hegemonic cultural structures.

In that sense, I think that there is a deep connection, because the Postmodern move—particularly in its "best mode,"—is about standing back from the modern social structure to take a critical vantage of it. So, in many ways, the kind of object of sociology is *society writ large*. And when you study *society writ large*, then you're sort of standing back from it and taking in an "objective" view. That is, you're taking society as an object of analysis and then trying to understand some of its features and its structures and its systems that maybe aren't readily apparent from within the context of society itself.

So, I think that the Postmodern move is very much about that shift of perspective. It's saying, *"All right, let's stand back from modernity, in particular, and let's examine how it functions. Let's look at the ways that economic systems and knowledge formation, and power structures and government structures in law influence the way that different group categories are even defined."* Or: *"Let's look at the medical system, or science, and examine how its particular paradigms might have given rise to notions of race or other kinds of socially-constructed categories that subsequently have been problematized or otherwise disrupted."*

And so, in that sense, I think that "woke" and "wokeness" can justifiably be related to the legacy of Postmodern critical interventions into sociological thought.

But in some ways it represents, at least to my mind, a sort of downward assimilated, popularized—you could even potentially say *bastardized*—version of that kind of analysis. It has been filtered down to college students, through academia. Once you got a generation, if not more than one generation, being pushed into higher education and presented with this set of ideas, it starts to filter through the rest of culture and permeate society more broadly.

ME: You've done a really good job of articulating, say, where things are today and how we got there. So, if I could maybe distill your message, you're articulating that there's been a "boiling down" effect of a larger Postmodern thesis and it has manifested itself today in the uninformed population as "Wokeism." Thus, it could be defined as a populist movement that leads to unintended consequences, since this reductionism leads to an identity-based stratification of very complex issues. Do you agree with that [breakdown]? Or perhaps you'd like to add some nuance to that point?

BRENDAN: Well, I'm always fond of adding nuance! But basically, that thesis I would agree with.

One of the frameworks that has become helpful for me to understand cultural trends is complexity and structuralism—*developmental structuralism* specifically. When you can take a developmental lens on culture and ideas, it becomes a very powerful way to understand how ideas from one level can get "downward assimilated" or watered down, or boiled down, however you want to frame that – "diffused" is usually another term I use. These ideas can get sort of *diffused* and watered down to a level of complexity that is actually much more simplistic compared to the level of complexity from which they originally arose. And that process leads to a great deal of information getting lost in translation.

Some of these ideas, which might be very valuable and important correctives in their more complex forms, when deployed in their more simplified forms are pathological and destructive. So, that would be the kind of 'unintended consequences' bit around this.

There's a lot I could say about that related to the developmental literature on some of these things because, real briefly, these ideas that emerge out of the Postmodern paradigm are really, I would say—many of them—valuable in their place, in their context, for doing the kind of work that they're trying to do. But to understand what they're originally trying to do requires the requisite level of complexity and development to appreciate entire social systems, to understand enough of history so that you can see how those have evolved through time and appreciate the broad swath of intellectual thought and the history of ideas. And, in their moment, they can fulfill a particular kind of critical function, which was actually really necessary.

But when you take those ideas, make them a paradigm of research and just teach them to 18-year-olds who are not developmentally prepared—or, I would also argue, *educationally* prepared—for that kind of material, then those ideas wind up being weaponized, simplified, and turned into simple clichés and stereotypes.

I think that most of what people are reacting to when it comes to 'wokeness' is essentially just that! So, yes, it has a kind of connection with the Postmodern movement, but it also in some ways represents the sort of simplified, toy version of Postmodern criticism that is very hard, to my mind, not to find incredibly unsatisfactory because it's missing so much complexity.

ME: Maybe we can focus on an example; I think that would be very useful for someone reading this.

So, I bring up in one of the chapters in my book (and this is a very simple example)—that Martin Luther King Jr. spoke poignantly in his famous "I Have a Dream" speech and mentioned that we ought to judge individuals by the *content of their character, not the color of their skin*. I argue that Woke methodology has essentially regressed from that statement. We are now almost universally and primarily judging people by the color of their skin and other identities that they associate with. I point out that this is a regressive nature of Postmodern thought, specifically Wokeism.

Speaking through that lens, do you feel like there is credence to that?

BRENDAN: Yes, 100%. The vision expressed by Martin

Luther King Jr. in that speech is very much of a fundamentally different sort than the kind espoused by woke ideologues. And I think that your analysis is basically right. What I do want to do, though, is try to throw in some of the nuance of *why that came to be*, and I think that's an important part of the story that can be missed because we're dealing with the downstream simplification of all of this.

What I think happened was basically this: when we don't take into account people's racial identities, we are missing important information, important contextual information that can actually wind up hurting those people. For example, if a qualified person has the experience of not getting hired for a job, the color of their skin may indeed be an important factor in understanding what happened there. More broadly than that, experiences of race in America are real and affect how people are brought up, how they live, what they value. We shouldn't ignore that.

This is where this notion of "color-blind racism" starts to enter in, which was a term that emerged to describe the hurt that can be done by *not* seeing the reality of race. People would say "I don't see color," but even if this is meant in the spirit of MLK, it can still negatively affect people. People who used this idea clearly still saw race, but they could sort of hide behind notions of not seeing race because we live in a "color-blind society." Stephen Colbert had a whole recurring bit about this dynamic back when he hosted *The Colbert Report*.

So, what happened was an attempt to lay that bare and say, "Hey, maybe it's actually kind of silly if we pretend like people aren't seeing race, because we all know that people *do* see race, and we're actually probably better off just acknowledging that."

When Black people in general get pulled over more by

police officers, for instance, but we want to say that we live in a colorblind society, how do we account for that? We have to take race seriously. We have to take into account the fact that people are recognizing that as an external marker that's significant to them, and I think that basic move is legitimate.

But what happened was that that message got diffused, simplified, watered down, and downward assimilated to rather simple-minded 18-year-olds. And so now we have clichés like the polemical term "color blind racism" itself, which can be deployed to counter just the sorts of moves MLK wanted to see happen in America. In fact, now just to even say what Martin Luther King, Jr said is actually deemed a form of racism by those folks! But that's obviously absurd.

We've lost so much of the information about what got us to this point that now we have flipped something on its head, and we don't even know how. Once things like that happen, it's very easy for them to get weaponized and used by people for their own kind of self-serving ends. Maybe in entirely unconscious ways, but that is the reality.

So, I think that an appropriate Postmodern move was to say, *"Hey, wait a second. Let's pay attention to race, because that's a sociological factor in understanding the situation."*

But then that trickles down through the system to the point where a college student may interpret this framework as, *"Oh yeah, race is the most salient feature about everyone. And everything's about power imbalances. So, all the white people are evil and stupid, and all the non-white people are the good guys."*

That's absurd. But the most important reason why is **this diagnosis lacks complexity.**

ME: I'll try to play back to you what I heard. The Postmodern framework, and specifically a lot of the tenants of Wokeism, are reductive in nature or a distillation of greater complexity. And college students and the populace at large distill the framework into non-meaningful forms.

What's beyond 'post-Postmodernism' with respect to Wokeism? How do we find an appropriate and valuable structure for culture synthesis?

What do you see? Is that the direction we're heading? Are we moving out of the negatives of Postmodern thought into a greater awareness of ourselves and our communities, including a more valuable representation for racism and all other 'isms' that are at play? If so, what is your evidence that we may be moving in that direction and moving beyond Wokeism to something greater, better, and more complete?

BRENDAN: What I write about in my *Metamodernism* book is the theory that these cultural moments occur when people take stock of what has been and then reflect on it, criticize it, and then attempt to move beyond it from a larger frame. And if you look at intellectual history in that way—even broad epochs from the Pre-modern to the Modern to the Postmodern—something like that seems to be what characterizes that shift.

So, you go back to the movement out of the Pre-modern era into the Modern era—and people like Petrarch, for example, had a very distinct awareness that they were doing something new and different. Petrarch even coined the term "dark ages" to refer to what had been before, and he had a new sense that there was this different way of being that was coming online.

But this continues into the so-called "debates of the Ancients versus the Moderns" in the early modern period.

It's a big debate in the early Renaissance of 'was the Renaissance period *better* than or even *equal to* the classical era?' Clearly there was a very intense, self-reflective awareness that what was happening in culture then could be compared to what had been before. And people were able to reflect on and critique and maybe even surpass what had been through this movement.

So, you see that happening in the movement from the Pre-modern to the Modern; and you also see it happening from the Modern into the Postmodern. As the name suggests, the Postmodern is very much a reflective awareness on Modernity itself—and taking it as an object and critiquing it reflectively, and trying to sort of extend the frame, move beyond the frame.

And so, what I propose is that Metamodernism is the same process unfolding, where now we have Postmodernism to stand back from, reflect upon, critique, and move beyond—and, not only that, we also are able to recognize increasingly that this is the process by means of which cultural evolution unfolds. So, from the Metamodern frame you have the awareness of these different cultural epochs and these cultural codes and different frames from the past: all as objects of analysis and reflection!

So, to your question: I am optimistic that as we move into the Metamodern era, we start to see the emergence of a distinctly Metamodern paradigm. We will see Postmodernism itself, and its associated "Woke Ideology," come to be an object of reflection, critique, and then ultimately transcendence.

Now I would say already, specifically, that we're clearly seeing that objectification and the critique. I mean, *"wokeness"* is a term that's on people's radar and people are responding to it very passionately and vehemently.

(Often, I would say, profoundly in a *reactive* way.) But this gets into some of the dialectical aspects we might touch on.

I just mention that because "Postmodernism" now, too, is very much in the air as a topic of concern, reflection, critique, and analysis. People like Jordan Peterson as well as certain prominent intellectuals have made this term a household phrase. So that now, today, *Postmodern* and *Woke* and other terms are being discussed and critiqued, and that's an important first step.

That is something we're already seeing. We're not just seeing the Postmodern paradigm being something that we're "swimming in"–which is more or less the case, I think, let's say over the past 40 years. Rather, now we've gotten to the point where we're able to step back from that and see that we've been swimming in a Postmodern paradigm and begin to reflect and critique that. We're already seeing big signs of that. I would say we're still in a relatively early phase of that.

Beyond that, I am very excited by developments in the Metamodern scene that seem to suggest what is to come. You're asking for specifics, so I'll point to the work of Hanzi Freinacht, who is the chief articulator of what he calls "Metamodern politics." Essentially, he's trying to articulate a developmental notion of politics and trying to appreciate that all of these cultural codes play a part in our social functioning in the political organism, and that we shouldn't demonize or antagonize any one of them in particular because they're all doing something important, even as we can recognize that maybe some are more complex than others.

I'll also point to the work of *The Institute of Cultural Evolution*, which does similar kinds of work, which applies a developmental lens to our political situation and sees through the lens of different value structures that are related to different sort of psycho-cultural structures with their own specific complexity levels. And when we can see that dynamic, we have a lot more tools to be able to navigate the culture wars rather than just see two sides yelling at each other. So, I've been really encouraged by their work. They're doing some very good things.

There are other people operating out of sort of this broad *milieu*—which you can call *developmental politics*. You could call it *Metamodern politics*. And the "integral theory" approach is definitely taken by a lot of people in this scene, influenced by the works of people like Ken Wilber and others. Stephanie Lepp, for instance, is doing some really interesting work trying to break apart the different values and narratives of different sides of the culture war, and rather than see them as simply antagonistic—or maybe one is right or wrong—trying to put them in dialogue with each other so that you can actually get a synthesis.

Similarly, the work of Jonathan Rowson, who's in the UK. He's recently received a Templeton grant to explore some work around different ways of doing dialogue and debate that isn't just crudely antagonistic, but somehow *synthetical*.

ME: These are great macro-level discussions and points you're making about the framework in general and its evolution and its eventual synthesis. But I often find that – at least with respect to how I've been writing this book – *examples* have the most proverbial "punch."

Is there a particular cultural divide or political topic that you're optimistic about, where the societal lens is shifting and at least the dialogue is becoming passable?

Let me give you an example. I have argued the term *"woke"*

has become the archetype of Postmodernism. And again, I think you've voiced that you may not fully agree—or at least there might be some nuance there. But of that archetype—that "poster child" of Postmodernism—*its* "poster child" has become the transgender movement. It's kind of the poster child of the poster child.

In today's political parlance and phraseology, one cannot even have a conversation about this topic without the pejorative "transphobe" thrown around instead of having a nuanced discussion about the binary nature of gender. So, the very language that we use in the current era is itself antithetical to free thought and discussion.

Do you see that changing? Or is there still a long way to go?

BRENDAN: Yes, I think it's already changing. I believe that the "woke wave" has already crested, really. I would say that we're on the other side of that now.

One demonstrable instance of that is the fact that large corporations are cutting or removing their legacy DEI programs. Walmart, just a couple of days ago, ended theirs, for instance, and a number of companies have quietly just stopped them altogether. And, generally, I think we're going to see over the coming years more of that sort of 'stepping back' from some of that more extreme ideological commitment from larger businesses. So that's a sign, I think.

Another sign, however much it might need to be interpreted, is the election of Donald Trump, which is clearly a repudiation of certain aspects of woke leftist thought. Again, that would really need to be unpacked, because it was presented as a simple binary—you know: Harris vs. Trump, and we got Trump. So, what does that really mean? But I do think some important ways of parsing the election and the reelection of Trump is as a kind of collective backlash against the kind of extremities of Wokeism.

But I do want to qualify all this a little bit, because I do think we're going to see two things, and we have to distinguish between them. What we're going to see is that there's definitely a move away from leftist, extreme woke ideology—*but* that could also be just owing to a rise of newly empowered reactionary thought, right? So that is not particularly compelling to me as a sign that we're moving forward; it could just be a sign that we've regressed even further. So, now, instead of kicking out the drag queens from reading to our kids in preschool, we're going to bring in Trump-praising pastors and other religious authorities to read them Bible stories and pray to them, right? This is already happening in Oklahoma. So, that's not a move ultimately in the direction that I would say is most salutary, but it does mark a shift *right* in terms of simply moving away from woke ideology.

I think in the future, we'll see aspects of each of these responses, and we'll have to disentangle them. And sometimes you can't necessarily disentangle them. Sometimes they'll be inherently mixed up with each other, so that people on a more authoritarian Christian nationalist bent will be pushing anti-woke ideology in a way that maybe other anti-authoritarian, libertarian-minded folks will get behind, ironically. You get a lot of strange bedfellows. I think you'll see that a lot in different political coalitions where people have shared goals but maybe different motivations and reasons in their pursuance of them. So, trying to read the tea leaves of the political moment is always going to be in some ways a matter of interpretation.

Where I am myself most optimistic, though, is in the new ways people are finding to talk about all of this, though it might seem a lot less sexy. It's not as policy-based and it's not inherently political in the typical sense, but simply having more ways of understanding the cultural phenomena that we're seeing—particularly developmental and complexity-based ways—is really encouraging to me, and I see more of that happening.

I see more people turning to those kinds of frameworks to make sense of things. I see more people being open to trying to speak across these differences in a kind of "meta" way that cognizes the polarities of the culture war, not as just a simple binary, but seeing multiple memetic tribes that all have particular values that they're trying to feed into the system as best they can. So, I see that kind of discourse increasingly coming online, and that's what most excites me. I think eventually that will start to trickle down and influence people and permeate society in a bigger way, too, just like Postmodernism did before it but, I think, ultimately in a more positive manner.

ME: Well, I'm equally optimistic as well. While writing this book, I brought up several analogies, including the chrysalis turning into the butterfly. And as a father of an 8-year-old, I've come to appreciate that metamorphosis is a part of life! And again, while this isn't a perfect analogy, I think our cultural epoch essentially is going to evolve and morph the way that a young biological child might. In the way culture went through Pre-modernity to Modernity, in much the same way my daughter went through infancy and becoming a toddler.

The Postmodern era is essentially puberty, and it is violent and clashing—and some may say regressive—but I think we're going to get through this. I'm thankfully not dealing with any of this yet with [my daughter] Ava; I have several more years, but I feel like after getting through that stage of her life that she'll be growing into a beautiful young adult who will then go on and achieve great things.

So, I believe that's what we're going through today. And I'm really excited about the evolution of our culture and its various layers that make it what it is. So, we'll see what the future holds; and I'll give you the last word. Thank you very much for speaking with me today, Brendan.

BRENDAN: Of course. I appreciate the invitation. Last word is – I would agree with that as a basic sort of metaphor; it's the one that I would hold to as well. I think it's not going to just happen automatically, though!

We do see regressions and breakdowns of civilization in the historical record. Romes can fall, and empires do collapse. And when they do, we lose complexity in a huge way that's been building up, and it takes centuries to regain that level of complexity.

So, what I'm hoping we can do is break through this period of chaos into a higher form of complexity rather than experience a breakdown to a more regressive mode. And both of those are very real options for us!

Developmental framings can be valuable, but it shouldn't lull us into a false sense of security because "this is just the dialectics of history inevitably leading to some goal that is sort of a foregone conclusion."

Rather, this is an active, participatory, always co-created society that we're a part of. It takes people changing the conversation and shifting the framework.

We need to update the shared cultural curriculum people

are responding to. So, books like the one you're writing and other things happening in the Metamodern conversation space are crucial, and I think self-consciously aware of having that role. So that's the best that we can do and what we can hope for.

Even if we see erratic changes and erratic movement, we shouldn't despair either. To return to Martin Luther King Jr for a second: *"The moral arc of the universe is long, but it bends towards justice."*

And we could say something similar about other aspects of cultural development, not just notions of justice—but our decency, our collective intelligence, and our collective problem-solving capacities.

I believe there is a certain kind of loose teleological orientation to the way that these things unfold, and provided we don't get in our own way, we can actually start working together to make a more complex future together.

We can see a better future! But it's not something that'll just arise spontaneously. We've got to do the work.

ME: Brendan, thanks so much for talking with me today. I really appreciate it.

BRENDAN: Thanks. It was a blast.

ABOUT THE AUTHOR

SEAN DEMPSEY

Sean is a husband, a father, an entrepreneur, a son, a poet, a friend, and — most recently — an author.

Focusing on a range of topics, Sean's narratives and philosophical insights are shared with a broad audience, encapsulating a journey from business landscapes to the tangible world of poetry & prose.

OTHER PUBLISHED WORKS

THE INVESTOR'S WARP WHISTLES

A financial tome which slaughters a lot of sacred cows. Learn why "normal" investing paradigms are 100% wrong! Discover the financial peace that comes when *PI > ME*.

www.WarpWhistles.com

A SAD COLLECTION OF SHORT STORIES

A bittersweet and ironic bevy of short stories and poems written between 2020 – 2023. This is a cathartic journey into the irrational state of "fearful man."

www.SadStories.net

THE SHUNT
A horror novella

My first attempt at a sci-fi/horror tale cast in the future. Learn the storied history of a technological device that has great promise … but also carries great risk.

www.ShuntBook.com

Made in the USA
Columbia, SC
30 December 2024

f4905d35-9968-4c29-9c37-afe51de61f80R01